Human Values and the Mind of Man

CURRENT TOPICS OF CONTEMPORARY THOUGHT

A series devoted to the publication of original and thought-evoking works on general topics of vital interest to philosophy, science and the humanities.

Edited by **Rubin Gotesky** and **Ervin Laszlo**

Volume 1

SYSTEM, STRUCTURE, AND EXPERIENCE. Toward a Scientific Theory of Mind
Ervin Laszlo

Volume 2

VALUE THEORY IN PHILOSOPHY AND SOCIAL SCIENCE
Proceedings of the First and Second Conferences on Value Inquiry
Edited by **Ervin Laszlo** and **James B. Wilbur**

Volume 3

INTEGRATIVE PRINCIPLES OF MODERN THOUGHT
Edited by **Henry Margenau**

Volume 4

HUMAN VALUES AND NATURAL SCIENCE. Proceedings of the Third Conference on Value Inquiry
Edited by **Ervin Laszlo** and **James B. Wilbur**

Volume 5

HUMAN DIGNITY: THIS CENTURY AND THE NEXT
Edited by **Rubin Gotesky** and **Ervin Laszlo**

Volume 6

HUMAN VALUES AND THE MIND OF MAN. Proceedings of the Fourth Conference on Value Inquiry
Edited by **Ervin Laszlo** and **James B. Wilbur**

Human Values and the Mind of Man

Proceedings of the Fourth Conference on Value Inquiry
State University of New York, College at Geneseo

Edited by

ERVIN LASZLO and JAMES B. WILBUR

GORDON AND BREACH SCIENCE PUBLISHERS
New York   London   Paris

Copyright © 1971 *by*

Gordon and Breach, Science Publishers, Inc.
440 Park Avenue South
New York, N.Y. 10016

Editorial office for the United Kingdom

Gordon and Breach, Science Publishers Ltd.
12 Bloomsbury Way
London W.C.1

Editorial office for France

Gordon and Breach
7–9 rue Emile Dubois
Paris 14ᵉ

Editors' Preface

The 4th Conference on Value Inquiry, on the topic *Human Values and the Mind of Man,* was called to examine how value questions have been treated in traditional theories of human nature, and to treat individual approaches to specific value questions in the context of contemporary philosophical psychology, exploring current directions and tendencies. Its suggested topics included the following: theory of mind as seen through the rules for the generation of languages; the implications for human value of automata theory; the nervous system, higher mental processes and human values; value consequences of various positions on the mind-body problem; the implications of self-actualization theory for human value; and specific value problems in the philosophy of mind. As can be seen from the breadth of the projected program, our intent was to hold an interdisciplinary conference the scope of which would extend to many of the leading areas in current thought about man, and yet center around their implications for human action, decision and the nature of what is traditionally referred to as the 'human mind.' It is our hope that the present volume, containing the proceedings of the conference, fulfills some of these expectations, and will promote the discussion of the ideas presented at the conference among a wider public of philosophers, psychologists, scientists and humanists.

The great schisms which still underlie contemporary theories of mind are clearly evident in the material presented in Part I, comprising the invited papers of the conference. The concept of mind as a locus of but dimly apprehendable properties, and the contrary notion, that the mind is adequately knowable in terms of behavior states and operational definitions, is contrasted in the contributions by J. B. Rhine, who exposes the still mysterious *psi* phenomena of parapsychology, the exploration of which he pioneered, and of B. R. Bugelski, who upholds the behaviorist view of a 'scientific psychology.' Ludwig von Bertalanffy, while deriving his concepts from a biological model, recognizes the supra-biological realms of mind. He places the locus of cultural values in a 'symbolic universe,' supervening over the universes of the non-living and the living. J. Wilder acknowledges the validity of the classical Freudian concepts and explores them in relation to values, drawing on his experience as a practicing psychoanalyst. Abraham Edel and Hermann Wein present philosophical treatises of mind and values; Edel focussing on the progressive disappearance of the concept of virtue from recent ethical theory, and Wein exposing a concept of mind in the light of contemporary continental trends in philosophical anthropology.

Part II, publishing the papers selected from among those submitted to the conference in response to its call for papers, opens with Larry Holmes arguing that humans set their own goals while machines do not, and thus no reduction of human ethical behavior to machines is possible. Next, Murray Greene subjects the meaning of hypnosis to a penetrating analysis in terms of Hegel's idea of Spirit. Some myths connected with the libertarian justification of free choice are exploded by Herman Tennessen; and Kenneth Haas argues that the concept of 'person' is properly a category of ethical and social thought and does not belong to the psychological analysis of individual consciousness and its content. Ruth Macklin, who also gave a paper at the first conference 1967, examines certain features of linguistic usage which are at the core of our attempts to develop a theory of action; and James King develops the position that ethics not only implies uniformity among men but actually enjoins it. Finally, Edward Sayles attempts to develop criteria for the meaningful critique of moral judgments within the context of a modified relativism.

The undersigned, directors of the conference and editors of this volume, wish to thank colleagues Gary Cox and William Edgar for their help in developing the program of the Conference, and to express their appreciation to Freda Hark for her assistance in preparing the manuscripts as well as the hundreds of small kindnesses *sine qua non*.

Ervin Laszlo
James B. Wilbur

Contents

PART I

Parapsychology and Man

J. B. RHINE

Institute of Parapsychology, Duke University

An attempt is here made to introduce the new branch of investigation, parapsychology, and to consider what it may contribute to our understanding of the nature of man. After a short sketch of this field, an outline of its relation to the main divisions of natural science will follow. As a third step the bearing of the new field upon the larger human disciplines will be illustrated. Finally attention will be focused on the role of parapsychology in a unified study centering on man's nature, a Science of Man.

Parapsychology

In 1927 a research program was begun in the Department of Psychology of Duke University under the sponsorship of Professor William McDougall, with the general aim of examining certain claims that man has powers that transcend his physical nature. Belief in the existence of such capacities was of course a very old one. They had, for example, been more or less implicitly assumed by most of the religions and magical systems. Rational support for this doctrine of a nonphysical element in man's nature had also been claimed in certain philosophical systems. The conventional sciences, on the other hand, confined as they are to sensory observations of physical phenomena, had not contributed anything definite to the support of this conception of the nature of man.

But even though the new program was committed to forthright search for possible nonphysical factors, it was nevertheless unreservedly restricted to the methodological principles of natural science; these of course would have to be adapted to the types of problem concerned, but it was assumed that the standards and canons of evidence already in use in the established sciences would be applied. Accordingly, it was a first requirement that the claims of exceptional powers to be investigated would have to be such as would lend themselves to controlled experimental procedures.

It was the claim of clairvoyant ability that proved to be the most suitable as a point of attack. This type of extrasensory perception (ESP) is an experience of knowledge of an object or objective event without sensory contact. An adequate test of this capacity would require that some reliable knowledge of the environment be obtained with all sensory mediation completely barred.

This type of test was comparatively simple and was easily conducted. As early as the 1880's the attempt had been made to adapt devices for acceptable testing procedures from current practices in the casinos; for example, ordinary playing cards could, when adequately concealed, serve as suitable targets for guessing tests of ESP of the clairvoyant type. Even the mathematics that had been developed for use in gambling proved suitable for estimating the extrachance significance of success in the card-guessing tests. Thus it was that this ancient belief in extrasensory powers of communication turned out to be ideally suited to the experimental laboratory. Not only could the ability to identify hidden cards be evaluated against the theory of chance coincidence, but any such performance could be carried out under conditions that completely excluded the entire range of the sense organs. Such was the testing for ESP which by this time has been under fairly continuous study for over 40 years.

The research program at Duke was not, however, strictly limited to the investigation of clairvoyance. On the basis of the test model used for that type of ESP a broader program of research developed, which became identified as experimental parapsychology—one that in due course spread to other centers here and abroad. Special test procedures were developed on generally similar lines, mostly for use with other types of ESP such as precognition and telepathy. Later they were developed, too, for the related ability involving extramotor response, which came to be called psychokinesis or PK, the direct action of mind on an external physical process or object. In due course all these types of parapsychical or *psi* ability, as they came to be called, were confirmed, first at the Duke Laboratory and later in other centers as well. Not only was the fact of their occurrence established but their common properties were explored and lawful relations discovered that established certain general principles applicable to all known *psi* phenomena.

However, the primary aim of the research program was focused steadfastly on the clairvoyance tests. By 1934 these had produced results under controlled test conditions repeatedly that could not be attributed to any known sense. Extrasensory perception at that stage was stated in this limited way, implying only that the *known* senses had been excluded. But as the program advanced into still more discriminating experimental conditions it became clear that there was no possibility of a sensory explanation of any type. On the basis of the results even the idea that a stimulus might be involved, as is always the case with sensory experience, had to be abandoned. As it became clear that ESP did not depend on any kind of sense or stimulus the more basic question of whether an essential physical process was involved could be brought to a decision. The conclusion was reached that no type of physical intermediation known to science could have produced the significant results obtained.

It seemed therefore safe to say that the original question of the research program had been answered. This did not mean that it was answered beyond all argument or that there was any alternative explanation to take the place of the physical and sensory mediation that had been excluded. Rather, this was simply the first step in a scientific inquiry, a step which eliminated the more familiar types of principle associated with the exchange between a person and his environment. The extrasensory and extraphysical type of exchange that remained had been established as experimentally real.

Naturally this conclusion was not reached in a single bound; nor was it based upon a single type of evidence. Rather, it was the culmination of years of investigation and the combination of a variety of types of evidence. The findings of the Duke Laboratory were confirmed at many other centers, but for that matter the work in parapsychology over the 35 years that have followed has yielded incidental confirmation too since of necessity it has all depended on the same basic *psi* operations that were established in the 1930's.

The conclusion that a nonphysical mode of exchange had been demonstrated was based on all of the types of ESP (and supported by other *psi* experimentation as well), but the one research line in which it was most obvious and most easily understood was that of precognition. This type of ESP ability had been demonstrated by tests in which the subject attempted to identify the order of targets *as it would be at a future time.* Then targets were carefully randomized and results independently checked, so that the precognition test was an ideally controlled one. In fact it has now been extensively used in parapsychology partly on this account and has been adapted to a variety of techniques involving in some cases electronic test machines, computerized analysis of results, and other modernizations.

But the point of importance here is that obviously no physical principle can furnish a reasonable explanation of the significant results obtained in the many years of precognition experiments; it appears therefore that this mental operation that transcends space–time requires a nonphysical type of agency to account for the effects produced. This fact as a scientific inference can stand alone even while the investigations continue in search for an understanding of the process.

What can we make of it?

At this point some cautious minds want to keep right on building larger and firmer structures of evidence for so radical a research finding that has so slowly been accepted. But fortunately others, not incautiously either, want to investigate the connections this *psi* occurrence may have with other 'departments' of nature. This too would have its reinforcement value since these interlocking discoveries would contribute to the rational structure of the science. In other words, while *psi* is partly established and defined by the discovery of what it is *not*—nonphysical, nonsensorimotor, nonconscious—it is not fully identified until its positive relations come into scientific view.

But there is still another reason to go on into these interrelations. *Psi* is difficult to capture; it is elusive and fugitive. It will likely become more controllable through studies of the psychology and biology of its operation. Such advances might pay off well in making it more successfully demonstrable and more rationally comprehensible.

Equally urgent however is the need to have the research adequately supported. This requires that some larger discipline appreciate the *psi* research field for its promise of usefulness and meaning; but increased knowledge and control of *psi* are necessary for that promise.

All this makes an almost perfect circle: (1) The basic *psi* research must be kept going. (2) This must however be broadened into related areas of science to improve control over the ability and to firm up its rationale; but (3) this 'interdepartmental' linkage requires strong financing for the more elaborate training and apparatus it needs. (4) This calls for a stage of assured application to justify the necessary support. (1) This step needs increased basic research (2) to improve control over the ability, and so on around again.

However this circularity disappears at once if we take the point of view, not of parapsychology itself, but the study of man as the larger unit to which *psi* belongs. This orientation leads as a logical next step to the question of how *psi* relates to the knowledge of nature man already knows through his sciences of physics, biology, and psychology —to take only broad divisions. In the section to follow a general answer to this question will be reviewed in the tentative way of a 'progress report.'

Relation to the main divisions of science

The relation of parapsychology to the main divisions of natural science is important because these connections are themselves part of the meaning of parapsychology for man and are even essential to the conception of parapsychology itself. In fact most of what we know about this field is in terms of its relations to other sciences. The investigator of *psi* must know something of its relation to physics in order to know *psi* itself; how much it belongs to psychology, and how it differs, are part of its very nature as a field; where it stands in the biological system is indeed fundamental parapsychology. All this is only to say we do not know any branch of science until we know its boundaries, and boundaries are themselves lines of interrelationships.

Fortunately there is no problem over the distinctiveness of the field of parapsychology. It has in fact a more clearly definable boundary line than many of the more established sciences. It deals only with *psi* phenomena and these are neatly identifiable as extrasensorimotor exchanges between persons and environment. But because of the nonphysical nature of these extrasensory and 'extramotor' interactions, they afford what is at present one of the most definite natural lines of division in the known natural order. This difference has been so impressive as to have led in the past to the categories of 'miraculous' and 'supernatural' in describing them (although not of course in parapsychology).

Physics

Parapsychology's first confrontation is logically with physics. As I have said, if *psi* phenomena had lent themselves to physical explanation they would not be *psi* phenomena—they would have been one of the many branches of the physical sciences. Even if they were conceivably to be accounted for by some dimly understood physical principle, some members of the vast professional population of the physical sciences today would have been vigorously pursuing such marginal prospects of extending present boundary lines of that field. But, as I have indicated, it has been possible to bring the matter to definitive experimental solution and it can therefore be regarded as decided, at least for the present stage of science.

But to find that *psi* is nonphysical does not entirely remove the process from relevance and interest to physics. The very act of demonstrating that an unknown type of influence is represented in *psi* exchange is dependent upon the physical system involved in the test and in the operation of the subject himself who takes it. This means of course that whatever *psi* is, it interoperates with the natural physical order. This necessarily implies the existence of a more general *common principle* as a basis of interoperation. Within the physical world itself, through which our scientific information is all intermediated, we know what is going on through the observation of physical events and through an inferential system built on that. Then too the instrumentation that has extended the range of the senses, of reasoning, and of memory has all been assumed to derive its causality from energetic systems. So long as only physical energetics was known there was thus no need to conceive of energetics as not necessarily *always* physical.

Now however we need to infer another kind of influence or energy that produces effects that are observable either directly or indirectly. The logic of natural science leads to the inference that a nonphysical influence is present that produces energetic effects. It becomes necessary therefore to infer from the results on record that an unknown energy is operating in the *psi* process. Since we do not know much yet about this hypothetical *psi* energy it is not a very big step to assume it. The concept will naturally become more realistic as we learn more about what the *psi* function is and can do, learn to control it better, and relate it to the rest of the natural order.[1]

Even now however physics cannot be regarded as the logically inclusive term it so long has been assumed to be. It is no longer the basis of *all* natural science and of the *entire* system of reality in the universe. In other words, we can now say the universe is more than physical—and that this is an experimental, not a merely speculative conclusion. It is therefore not just a matter of viewpoint, although it will require a fundamental shift in some categories. For example, energetics has been considered a branch of physics; now it will have to be the other way around, with physics subordinate to energetics, since a nonphysical mode of causality is required in *psi* communication.

A few physicists at least are already interested in this energetic interconversion between *psi* and physical energy. Like some of the familiar energies, *psi* can only be detected through conversion to directly registrable readings of another energetic form. For example, it is only as some observable physical process can be influenced by PK that this type of *psi* function can be manifested and measured. But this transfer, like the types of ESP too, is now experimentally manageable, and it opens a new frontier for the research physicist. He can for instance do something that has hitherto been considered impossible: He can react experimentally to a future event and he can interact directly as from one mind to another (no matter as yet what a mind is!). He can exert intelligent influence on bodies without contact, and with no known physical field to intermediate. But in all this the researcher in physics would not necessarily be going entirely out of his own field to investigate parapsychological interaction. Physics is not just the study of inanimate bodies as an older academic viewpoint may have had it. In a modified way it is biophysics, psychophysics, and of course *psi*-physics too.

One can look back through the history of physics and see that such changes have always come hard, but they eventually occur. This 'expanding' universe we know about today is not the same one Einstein was thinking about, any more than his was like Newton's. 'If it (ESP) does not relate to space-time it must be wrong,' Einstein was quoted as having said on his first reaction to the early report on the ESP research. To be sure, this only meant that it 'must be wrong' for the prevailing conception of a strictly physical universe, which he like his generation had been educated to accept as the entirety of nature. Now, with ESP established, the concept of the universality of physics has to be shelved. This should be a great relief, since that concept has been a heavy burden on the rational mind of man for a century or more, even persuading many that such a 'mint' was either unreal or impotent.

Biology

Since *psi* communication is known only in connection with living beings, parapsychology logically belongs to biology. In view of what is known today about the distribution of spontaneous cases suggesting *psi* capacity in other species than man, one might suppose that parapsychology could well enough have had its origin in observations of the behavior of lower animals. Apparently instances of such unusual behavior have always been current, but biologists like psychologists have given them no attention. The challenge such cases offered to physical explanation has been as much of a deterrent consideration in biology as in psychology.

However, once *psi* ability was found to be widespread in the human species, attention was directed to the reports of similar ability in animals, and as with man it was the spontaneous happenings that served as the starting point. The most familiar animal performance that seemed in some cases extrasensory is that of long distance homing. Still more suggestive of *psi* ability, though less frequent, are the cases of what is called *psi-trailing,* in which a pet animal finds its way to a new location after it has been left behind at the time the family moves. With long distances involved and with good identification of the animal, some of these cases can be impressive. Also, in many instances the reaction of pet animals, especially dogs, to the death or serious illness of a human companion, sometimes many miles away, has strongly suggested ESP. Sometimes too the apparent anticipation of impending danger has been well indicated by appropriate behavior.

Such cases have led to experimental study of ESP in a few of the species more convenient to work with (*e.g.* dogs, cats, pigeons, and mice) and the confirmatory evidence is amply adequate to warrant the growing interest in this branch. One university laboratory of zoology has in recent years launched a program of research and has reported (albeit under assumed names) evidence of ESP in mice, obtained in fully automated testing.

While the work on *psi* in animals (*anpsi*) is being continued it has already advanced far enough to justify consideration of some of its consequences. In the main the anpsi results fit in well with the larger background of better-established findings from the human species. Taken together, there is enough coverage for some useful exploratory generalization regarding *psi* and the science of life.

For example; one immediately suspects that the point of origin of *psi* must have been far back in evolutionary history, long before man himself arrived. It follows that there is a need for a more comparative study of *psi* in different species, to see whether there has been progress or decline of *psi* ability with evolution. In the background of such a search for evidence of *psi* in different species there will always be the pertinent question as to what the value of this ability has been to biological survival.

The practically oriented *psi* worker will turn hopefully to these comparative studies with the desire of finding a species suited to selective breeding and other genetic studies of the *psi* function, aiming eventually at the discovery of an ideal experimental 'guinea pig.'

Limited though *psi* research has mainly been in the past to the human species, certain biological generalities have emerged that afford a tentative base line for interspecies comparisons. For instance, no relation of *psi* ability to age has thus far been noted, no true difference between the sexes—in fact, no fundamental difference between any biological group. Even though these observations have been incidental and not yet based upon designed studies, they have considerable tentative value. Also some importance can be attached to what has *not* been found. For example; there has been no indication of a localization of exchange, no port of entry or exit for *psi* interaction to compare to the senses and muscles. There has been no suggestion of special localization of the essential *psi* process itself within the nervous system. This fact along with the nonphysical character of the *psi* operation raises the question whether there will ever be found a physical center of the kind involved in the sensorimotor exchange. This is an area on which comparative animal studies might introduce some new ideas on possible somatic correlates of *psi* (as well as of course psychological correlates).

While it is yet too early to entertain more than tentative judgments about the general biology of *psi,* the elementary insights already acquired seem to bear on some of the major unsolved problems in biology. Consider first that parapsychology introduces biology to a new energetic influence to add to its basic principles in the study of the nature of life. Already there are enough experimental indications to justify relating the *psi* factor to the forces involved in growth, in health, and in a range of psychosomatic relations. At least it should be considered as a matter for research. It should not therefore be surprising that in view of the vast amount of PK research on moving (inanimate) targets that the few controlled studies of its effect on *living* tissues have given positive results (mostly but not entirely on plants). This of course brings us to the frontiers of medicine, and that discipline for all its restrictive reticence regarding the unorthodox is rich in its backlog of fascinatingly baffling cases, many of which seem undoubtedly to belong to parapsychology. Because of the great human importance of this medical frontier of biology it seems likely that it will serve as the main impetus for the future study of '*psi*-biology.' In fact medical parapsychology is likely to lead the way for this new field much as medical psychology and the branches of medical biology have done for the basic sciences in the past.

A few of the main types of cases will illustrate what medicine has long been storing away in its cupboards of unorthodox cases: One thinks of the many puzzling twin cases (that so rarely get reported).

For example, a pair of twin schizophrenics, separated, locked in different hospital wards, spontaneously died at the same hour the night following their forced separation. The autopsy revealed no cause of death. Another case-type is that of mothers who experience very realistic birth pains simultaneously with their daughter's (who in one case was on another continent) as the latter was actually giving birth to a baby. A third type: A woman about to have a baby told the doctor correctly it would have only one hand, because its father lost a hand in a mine accident. A Duke student dreamed her soldier-fiancé in Italy had white hair and wrote him. The night he landed on Anzio Beach his hair did turn white. The dermatologist of course said it was impossible. But new sciences rather commonly germinate from the 'impossibles' of the old—if they are reported.

For the present the main impact of parapsychology upon biology (and it will likely be most effective with medical biology) is likely to be in giving encouragement to the reporting of the puzzling cases that are encountered in practice. The parapsychologist is now a 'specialist' (at least in research) to whom these odd problems may be referred. As it is he is being consulted frequently by a few practitioners, mainly psychiatrists, who are led to suspect a *psi* element in the patient's problem.

Meanwhile parapsychology will keep the initiaitve it has taken in following up such opportunities and helping to bridge the gap of knowledge it has with the biological system of nature. It seems likely at present that it will make its best contact with biology over the pile of problems that might be called 'parapsychosomatic.' These are cases that combine what seems like a mentally induced illness based on a telepathic response to a loved one's trouble (like the birth-pain case mentioned above). The research into this area can best be started by the *psi* worker but it should lead to a convergence of several scientific specialities, and this is part of its advantage. The psychiatrist may be more ready to assist than others, and he might be expected to take the lead in meeting the challenge these cases present.

Psychology

It is fairly obvious that parapsychology has more in common with the field of psychology than with any other branch of science. By most definitions of psychology it would even have to be considered a subdivision. However, the field of psychology, like most of the others, developed under conditions in which practical requirements for teaching within the university placed limits on what was acceptable. Psychology (like the field of biology to which it technically belongs) had to meet academic rules and standards largely determined by the more easily operated physical sciences. The standards of demonstration, interpretation, and publication tended to follow as closely as possible the better established physical branches of inquiry. Even the universe came to be regarded by academic science as physical, and good scientists sought only for physical principles of explanation. Whatever else there may have been in the sciences of biology and psychology that did not lend itself to these criteria of intellectual status in the academic marketplace were just not brought forward and developed. Natural selection operates among ideas too.

It is understandable then that because it has so much in common with psychology, parapsychology has constituted a threat to the university psychologist who was striving to keep his field as much like the prevailing academic style as he could. Most of the friction between these fields derived from attempts to push parapsychology prematurely into psychology departments. The same thing would have happened to psychology itself if it had been originally forced into departments of biology instead of, as it was, into those of philosophy and education.

As a matter of fact the only line that marks parapsychology off from the rest of the general field is the extrasensorimotor character of its operation. This seems at present like a very sharp line of differentiation, but that impression may well be the result of our limited knowledge of the actual borderline of the sensorimotor. (Most boundary lines in science have tended to dim with growing knowledge.)

The most distinctive finding of parapsychology as things now appear is the nonphysicality of its phenomena. These are the only occurrences known to the psychological sciences that have lent themselves to a crucial test of this hypothesis. Many people have thought there is or might be something nonphysical about the human mind, even apart from religious theories; but obtaining scientific proof on the point is another matter. Psychologists of certain schools have conceived of mind and body as two different orders of reality. Perhaps the most explicit on this matter was William McDougall, as represented in his *Body and Mind* in 1911. He felt he was supported in his position by the evidence of parapsychology even as it was then. A more conclusive statement of the role of parapsychology in establishing the reality of mind came out over 50 years later from another British psychologist, John Beloff, in his book *The Existence of Mind*.

By this time it seems safe to say that the issue has been drawn by parapsychology and settled on an adequately scientific basis. When in due course psychology becomes free enough in its academic position to take an independent stand it will have a sound empirical basis for a claim to a real and independent territory of its own. So long as it is limiting its subject matter to operations that do not defy physical explanation it is in actual practice just a subdivision of the physical sciences. Now however it has title to the *psi* research findings that, small as they are as yet, stand clear of subordination to physical explanation. Probably this gift is at first about as welcome as something the cat dragged in; but its ultimate importance is likely to be proportional to its initial nuisance value.

Far more immediately important to psychology however is what *psi* adds to its exploratory coverage. In the past a psychologist has been limited to his own self-imposed mechanistic thinking. Watson and Lashley, for example, on going out to study the migratory flight of the sooty tern, quite logically stated that they were seeking explanations within the range of the sensory functions of the birds. If the birds should have been using ESP the observers would have overlooked it. Parapsychology on the other hand has exemplified the scientific procedure of trying to solve the problem, whatever the answer turns out to be. It is searching for any reliably demonstrable explanation of a phenomenon that is actually there in nature. It has, without previous commitment, without any hand-tying assumptions, demonstrated that the methods of science are dependable without such confining restrictions as a behaviorist or physicalist conception of science might impose.

What seems likely to have the greatest longterm consequence for psychology is the fact that parapsychology gives a degree of causal potentiality to the mental system to which *psi* belongs. As I have said, science in the past has invariably applied the term energetic to demonstrated causality, and now the concept of a mental energy is available for the use of the psychologist and with a more authentic basis today than it has ever had in any similar usage in the past. While it is true the concept that the mind has a real force that is not physical will seem to many a very revolutionary change so long as the habit of equating energetics to physics stand in the way, the results of *psi* research must eventually be reckoned with.

The body-mind problem may be regarded as partly solved by the fact of the nonphysical nature of *psi*. This rules out at once certain hypotheses and brings causal interaction to a state of confirmation. What seems most reasonable to suggest is that this introduces a useful experimental approach and opens up a new research area centering around the greatest intellectual gap in modern science, the thought-brain interaction. The establishment of mental causality and the techniques of parapsychology should give the sciences that are involved an effective new grasp of this problem area.

The concept of mental causality as a natural influence to be worked with and engineered is one the world of human affairs is awaiting, coasting as it has been on outworn belief-systems that have lost their potency. Now, in education, psychotherapy, ethics, law, and in many other areas of urgent importance today, psychology can be prepared to take a new approach. It can now be confident that there is a determinacy that is potential in the human mind, which was not developed merely to influence the fall of dice in a PK test or make predictions across barriers of space-time in ESP experiments. Anything lawful enough to be repeatedly demonstrated under test conditions must be supposed to be operative in nature, and it is the research task of the larger field to explore the range, the capacity, the full possibility of the development of this power peculiar to the mind itself.

There is no actual conflict between the *psi* results and psychology as a science. There is only the addition of a wider range of ability—an extremely wide range indeed in its full potential; the extrasensorimotor with which parapsychology deals is in one respect just another zone of communication, even though it is based on a different underlying principle. Furthermore, although psychology will now in due course become psychocentric again, this will not lessen the achievements of its more cerebrocentric (and physicalistic) phase; but it will extend its perspective of exploration and permit a much wider range of problems to be handled. When psychology becomes accomodated to the findings of parapsychology it will neither be justifiable to restrict inquiry to sensorimotor action alone nor confine explanation to physical principles. With such an expanded franchise this most urgently needed of all the divisions of science may realize more of its great potential for the understanding and control of the planet's most troublesome species.

Relation to religion

It follows that if parapsychology has contributed evidence of a non-physical principle in man's nature that it will in consequence of this fact alone affect all those many social institutions and disciplines which depend upon a concept of man. This is not to overlook the fact that we know so little as yet about *psi* itself that it will be a long time before the nature and extent of these consequences will become known. But even on the basis of what we know already about it, the mere knowledge of the occurrence of *psi* will make a difference in the concept of what a man is and therefore in what every organization of men will be.

If this were not so obviously a logical consequence it would be necessary to go over the whole range of the major human institutions and review one by one the relevance of parapsychology for each particular organization. Of course they will not all be equally involved, and there will be differences in receptivity to the findings of *psi* research and in the readiness to adopt them. In terms of need one thinks first of such systems as mental health, education, the ethical institutions, and medicine. These to a great extent are waiting for a better validated theory of man's nature. Without it they are caught in the uncertain transition from one unvalidated belief system to another.

On this occasion however I can deal with only one of these larger social disciplines as an example of what parapsychology will conceivably mean to human institutions as a class. And for this purpose I have chosen religion. It will better serve the purpose because it is closer to the field of parapsychology than any other major social institution, and because it is more transparently dependent upon a theory of man. The truism that the way we treat people depends upon what we think they are is particularly manifest in religion.

What now has parapsychology really to do with religion? It is rather like the relation of biology to medicine or of physics to engineering, except that the relation in this case is still but little recognized. As a matter of fact parapsychology has developed quite independently of professional religious influence; and even today there is no official relationship or recognition existing between the two fields.

Therefore all such relationships as I shall be pointing out are rather abstract; for example, parapsychology in its refutation of the philosophy of materialism has a very obvious bearing on religion; materialism has probably been religion's greatest enemy. Moreover, the discovery of *psi* as a nonphysical property of man is science's first positive contribution to religion. In the long warfare between science and religion since the 16th Century nothing like this ever happened before. Yet this contribution has never thus far even been recognized by any organized religion. For that matter no great point of it has been made in parapsychology either; as I have said, there has been little exchange between parapsychology and religion.

However a curious interrelationship has been found: What parapsychology had discovered and labeled *psi* communication in all its types, forms, and conditions has turned out to have a remarkable parallel to the whole communication system of religion—that is, to the modalities of exchange that have been assumed to occur between the human and the divine orders. Or, putting it conversely, men have been assuming in their religious doctrines a pattern of communication between men and their deities that coincides almost exactly with the types of exchange between a person and his environment that have been developed by parapsychology. In still other words, had the founders of the religions been working with the 34 volume set of the *Journal of Parapsychology,* or had the workers in parapsychology been guided by the scriptures of the great religions, the parallelism of the two systems of communication could hardly have been more nearly perfect. This is the more remarkable in view of the independence of the two disciplines from each other throughout.

A brief outline will indicate this congruency of patterns. Parapsychology has revealed the existence of an extrasensorimotor order of exchange between a person and his world. On the extrasensory side the types of phenomena verified are the clairvoyant, telepathic, and precognitive. On the other are the psychokinetic; the PK effect has been demonstrated first on moving objects, second (to a considerable extent) on living targets, and it is being investigated on a third 'state of matter,' static inanimate targets.

When we turn now to the types of communication assumed in a (generalized) religious system we find they are identical in principle, even though not as sharply distinguished and exemplified. Beginning with the powers attributed to divinity the terms omniscience and omnipotence are essentially equivalent to extrasensory perception and psychokinesis, allowing an assumption of perfection that of course goes with deification. On the human side of the religious exchange one sees at once the similarity of precognition to prophecy, of telepathy to prayer, and of clairvoyance to revelation, seership, and related mystical experience. On the physical side of the exchange the types of psychokinetic interaction are well exemplified in the varieties of physical manifestation furnished by the miracles.

This similarity is quite as remarkable when it comes to the states or forms of experience in which communication with the divine order occurs. In *psi* research these have been found most commonly to be dreams, hallucinations, intuitions, and unexplainable physical manifestations. These are the standard classifications of the mode of experi-

ence of spontaneous *psi* occurrences. But they also serve equally well
as the classifications of the way in which spontaneous religious manifestations are experienced, the forms in which messages are believed to
be received from the divine order. The parallel continues on into the
type of practices that have developed along with the religions, the
trances, and other special dissociated states induced in preparation for
the religious experience. The point of similarity that emerges here is
that just as with *psi* ability today, so for the exercise of religious communication, there was little conscious control possible. The capacity
was (and is) elusive and fugitive. It is a delicate mode of exchange.

What emerges from this study is that we have a modern confirmation
of patterns of communication that have grown up through the ages in
the systems of the various religions. Whatever else may be said about it,
it would appear that the founders of the various major religions were to
a remarkable extent following a pattern of reality of human experience
that is now today independently substantiated as having a valid basis.
The essential similarity of these basic patterns extending throughout
the various theological doctrines adds generality to the picture as well.

It is not necessary to elaborate here the many new roads to further
scholarship opened by this isomorphic relationship of *psi* communication to religious communication. We can leave this further interest to
what is on the way to becoming a new course of study and research—
the Parapsychology of Religion.

What may be most worth suggesting about this relationship of parapsychology and religion is that it would seem to be comparable to the
stage in the history of those disciplines at which science has already
gained a foothold. The most obvious illustration is the reformation of
medicine with the discovery of the circulation of the blood, or perhaps
more clearly with the germ theory of disease. It would appear that parapsychology could be expected now with its contribution to the understanding of religious communication to have exemplified the relationship of a basic science to a field of application—a relationship in the
making. What this will mean to religion will have to be left to the
future, but it should mean something to have discovered that men
themselves have those very powers that they once attributed to divinity
and which they believed (as they once did all natural principles) to
belong to the supernatural. As we all know, most of the things men are
doing for themselves today are being done because they discovered the
natural principles which their ancestors had deified. It looks very much
as if the world may have reached the stage at which people must learn

to do a great deal more for their own personal and social guidance that they have hitherto left to the supernatural.

The science of man

There is a third relationship of parapsychology to be considered. I have discussed its relation to the divisions of natural science, and to the larger human disciplines, as exemplified in religion. But neither of these relations point up what is, I think, its peculiarly relevant bearing. For this it needs more centralized involvement, the more integrated setting identified with the focus of study of the nature of man. For one thing, it is likely to be a long time before the sciences allow themselves to be very much awakened to the significance of *psi* for their particular 'departments' of the universe. They all have heavy preoccupations of their own.

And as for the greater human disciplines, while it does appear that the world is being rudely shaken out of its complacency concerning its social institutions and value systems, I do not anticipate any beating of paths to the doorsteps of the parapsychology laboratories to get help from them on remodeling a theory of man.

Rather, such a message as parapsychology had acquired is novel and different enough that it needs its own launching organization (just as it does its own research centers) for its proper exploitation. Rather than losing itself in adapting to other essentially dissimilar areas, it needs to draw into and around itself the buttressing organization of related interests needed to make its potential more realizable and manifest.

By far the most revolutionary consequence of the findings of parapsychology are in what they contribute to the understanding of man's nature. But taken alone and taken at this stage this contribution is and may long remain a rather impotent germ, whatever its ultimate potential. It needs, therefore, to be made part of a composite science devoted to the understanding of the distinctive nature of man. Such a science of man cannot be merely a parapsychological one nor can it even be completely psychological, even in the broadest conception of that over-limited term. Rather it will have to be biological too in so many features that it would be difficult to characterize the range of the sciences of life involved as this convergent science grows to maturity. But for that matter it would be equally impossible to conceive of the science of total man as not being firmly structured into a close interrelation with the framework of physical science, and with a broader science of energetics that embodies all that scholarship can encompass. For 'man is the measure of all things.'

Such a design for the study of man as a person needs to begin with parapsychology only because it is farthest out; only this will insure that the new branch will not be lost under the pressures of accomodation to the stronger fields that are so well reinforced with the sinews of research. With parapsychology entrenched as a fundamental branch of the research program it will have the necessary advantage of orientation. Here at one place in the world of research will man's nature be explored as fully as possible in all those relations that harmoniously integrate in a scientifically discoverable way. There will be no blocking limitations arising where *psi* (or whatever else may be discovered) has to interrelate with branches that are dominated by biased assumptions.

It does not really matter that at present parapsychology seems to represent a small image placed on a high pedestal. If mankind in its various systems of religion deified these curious *psi* aspects of human personality as they did, it is not inconceivable that science will make more of the matter in due course than even the imaginative founders of the religions did, just as they have made more out of the principle of the uncertain capricious agency that once was called Jove's thunderbolt. At least, after all the other things men have done and have created, it would now seem timely to launch a major research program aimed strictly at man himself, with a starting focus on the powers the ancients in all their cultures most exalted.

Note

1. What is the criterion of an energetic effect? For this stage it is the statistically significant evidence of communication between person and environment that has been adequately confirmed. Energy is required to alter those elements of the test situation that tend to produce chance results.

Reism and the Status of Mind in Scientific Psychology

B. RICHARD BUGELSKI

State University of New York at Buffalo

More than half a century has passed since John B. Watson, in 1913, proclaimed the principles of Behaviorism as a program for psychologists who would presume to consider themselves scientists. His program was modeled on already flourishing scientific operations in the realms of physics and chemistry. The proper study of mankind was to be based on observation of external reality, of objects in motion, of man behaving. Only repeatable observations of organisms in motion, repeatable by anyone, would be acceptable as data. There had to be a social check. Data from self-observation, not subject to the social check, were unacceptable. Introspection on sensations, images, and feelings was outlawed.

When Watson struck down sensations, images, and feelings, he was both logically and psychologically correct. There are no such *things* as sensations, images, feelings. These terms are, at best, abbreviations for material functions of material bodies. Watson, of course, did not deny reactions of sense or body organs to stimulation or to operations of the nervous system. While he did deny images, for example, images could be translated as they were by Leuba (1942) into conditioned activation of sensory processes once elicited by appropriate physical stimulation. Neural processes are things in action and consequently permissible objects of study. For a while the psychological world began to act as if it had learned the lesson; it stopped talking about instincts, ideas, thoughts, wills, intelligence, and a host of other nouns which had up until then been the subject matter of psychology and began to talk in verbs, participles, and adjectives, for example 'intelligent behavior.' This effort was a partial step in the right direction but it still assumed the debatable existence of behavior as a thing. There are only behaving things to be studied—behavior, *per se,* is also unobservable. There is no such thing.

While some of the more theoretically oriented psychologists responded favorably to Watson's radical objectivism, most psychologists could not completely give up their allegiance to some presumed internal agencies or mechanisms which they regarded as either personally self-evident in some cases, or as logical deductions from certain observations. Thus, to take a simple example: given persons A and B, both faced with the same problem, with A succeeding and B failing in arriving at a solution, it follows that A is superior to B and must somehow possess something that makes him superior; perhaps A has a superior mind to that of B. Because other observations led to the deduction of other attributes of mind, success in problem-solving is taken as evidence of an attribute or factor of intelligence in a mind. Such deductions are apparently quite commonly accepted by laymen, teachers, and even some professional psychologists who endow persons not only with intelligence, but other skills, traits, capacities, attitudes, personalities, ids, egos, super-egos, consciences, values, anxieties, and a whole Pantheon of forces, features, and functions.

References to some hypothetical mind were, of course, obnoxious to Watson and his behavioristic successors. Not only did they reject any such structure as a mind, long and still favored by most philosophers, but they also rejected any of its alleged attributes or processes such as consciousness. The Freudian Unconscious was equally considered anathema as it too postulated some kinds of subjective, mentalistic processes which had no substantive physical basis.

Most psychologists writing today act as if they do not appear to recognize that if a person solves a problem, the only thing that is observed or can be observed is that he arrives at a solution. The desire to hold fast to an orderly world and find a cause for everything then prompts the act of putting into the problem solver a problem-solving agency. The intelligence now postulated is just that, postulated. It has not been observed. Every so often it becomes necessary to remind the psychological world of Watson's *dicta.*

Another person does something in some regular and frequently observable way—*e.g.* he smokes cigarettes or drinks a lot of coffee or tugs at an ear lobe. Observers are wont to say: he has a habit of smoking, drinking, tugging, or what-not. All that has been observed is the frequency of some behavior sample. Nobody ever saw a habit. Yet even so astute and objective a psychologist as Hull (1943) was quite eager to postulate a hypothetical construct of habit, identified symbolically as s H r, and presumed to exist in potentially observable form at some future time. Hull did appreciate that the construct was imaginary until established physiologically. The danger exists, however, that some imaginary constructs will always remain so because there is no underlying physiological structure. Such constructs can only retard science. In any case, a habit could never be seen. It could not be a thing like a carburetor. At best one might be able to point to some neural structures that were somehow different from what they were prior to the formation of the 'habit.'

Bad habits too can be talked about 'scientifically' as inferences from observations, reflecting something allegedly inside the performer. The process of theorizing about habits, drives and motives, inhibitions, *etc.*, can be made to appear even more scientific by adopting various practices such as those suggested by the operationists who require rigorous descriptions of procedures in arriving at definitions of concepts. But almost any kinds of operations can be described and their consequence presented as definitions of something. Commonly this definition refers to a thing when there is no thing and the process inevitably results in reification of a non thing. Psychologists eagerly jumped on the operationist's band-wagon and tried to drive it in all sorts of directions. But, bad operationism does not make a science.

Dr. Joseph B. Rhine provides us with a perfect example of the practice of generating a thing by procedural definition. He describes his procedures and can do so most objectively. As a result of his procedures, he arrives at scores from which he chooses to infer the existence of forces or energies not observable or manipulable in themselves. Dr. Rhine has not observed ESP or PK—he has created them, just as others have created habits or intelligence through a process of description with the result that they appear to be things when there are no such things to begin with in any sense as concrete objects. Whatever Dr. Rhine is doing, he is not working with a real world. He is not experimenting as he has no way of setting up controls by withholding ESP. There is no thing to withhold. For any thing to be other than a concrete object should at least perplex one. The tender-minded will be disturbed by this rejection of some of their most treasured constructs. The desirability or gratification provided by these constructs is no testimonial to their reality.

A more sophisticated approach was that developed by Edward C. Tolman (1937) who applied mathematical terminology (functions) to measurements obtained in observing animals under a variety of conditions. Tolman styled himself a behaviorist and called his procedure that of working with intervening variables. According to this view, one could measure the activities of organisms with some scale or procedure, get scores, and note the relationship between these scores and other activities. Thus if a score, I.Q. (*not* intelligence), showed some relation to the speed of problem solving, such a score could be considered a predictor of the speed or the speed could be considered a mathematical function of the score. All thinking about or operating on such scores would follow the rules of mathematics and logic and in effect, follow the rules of a grammar of science. We have no quarrel with mathematics, logic, or grammar. They deal with signs, symbols, or words; and words are never things except as they may be seen as ink on paper, or heard as noises.

We return now to Watson and recognize that Watson did more than try to do away with subjective or self-observation. He was following an earlier tradition, traceable to the Greeks, but showing up more specifically in the writings of Avenarius and Leibnitz in their nominalistic philosophies. Both Avenarius and Leibnitz were concerned about the nature of the real world and its inhabitants, creatures and things. They wanted to discover and deal with only what was real even though they were dualists. Watson was a materialistic monist and wanted to work only with the material world of the senses. He simply did not go far enough. He managed quite effectively to get rid of minds, images, ideas, and other mentalistic mechanisms but he retained far too many non-real materialistic mechanisms, *e.g.* emotions, reflexes, habits, the very foundations of his system. So used are we to this manner of working (we all acquire similar vocabularies) that none of us is free from occasionally, if not regularly, falling into verbalistic traps and acting as if things that do not exist actually do.

Today B. F. Skinner (1953) regards himself as a stalwart Behaviorist and does, indeed, improve on Watson's language. Skinner will have nothing to do with what he calls 'linguistic fictions' and stringently avoids reference to anything that cannot be seen or measured. In a similar vein D. O. Hebb (1949) presented a thoroughly objective psychology of a reductionist nature by translating alleged subjective entities into purely physiological processes. For Hebb, for example, an idea is nothing but, and certainly no more than, the discharge of a certain number of neural elements. An allegedly subjective experience that might be labeled an 'expectancy' is simply the firing of some neurons prior to their normal reaction to some originally specific stimulus because of the arousal of some neural circuit in what amounts to a premature activation.

Much of what is talked about in terms which are linguistic fictions, however, can be talked about in other words, words that do refer to things. To do so is frequently difficult and almost calls for a new language. In his book *Verbal Behavior,* Skinner (1957) had to invent many new terms to discuss the actions of people when talking simply to stay in the world of the real. The language of Skinner and his followers frequently sounds like circumlocution and commonly calls for translation into terms with which a listener is more comfortable, even though deluded.

The psychological systems described by behavioristically inclined psychologists in the 50 years since Watson's Prologomena have all been variously successful attempts at working within a framework that has been described by the eminent Polish symbolic logician and philosopher Kotarbinski (1966) as the philosophy of Reism or Concretism. From the reistic or concretistic point of view much of our language, ordinary or scientific, consists of words referring to alleged properties or relationships which are not things. When we talk of mental states like consciousness or of so-called events, we are not dealing with material substances and when we leave the world of substance we lose contact with reality. We can only return through a process of translation and all too commonly we lose much in the translation.

Floyd Allport, the social psychologist who first attempted a behavioristic social psychology in the late '20s, made the same point in his paper on Institutional Behavior (1947) some years later when he exposed the emptiness of such terms as 'the Government,' 'the University,' 'the Court', showing them to be as empty of meaning and distressingly confusing. In Franklin Delano Roosevelt's second term that astute politician and realist saw through the smoke screen that obscured the real meaning of the work of the Supreme Court of that day. He referred to the 'nine old men' who were frustrating his efforts at social legislation. Unfortunately for him the general public was (and is) in love with its Sacred Cows and Roosevelt suffered a political set-back because he dared to tell the truth. The public was not ready to recognize that the Supreme Court consisted of some rather cantankerous and reactionary superannuated citizens.

Kotarbinski asserts that words referring to relationships, minds, mental processes, institutions, and various 'isms' are, at best, abbreviations for what would require many extended statements, paragraphs or chapters, before they could be translated back into a contact with reality. Without such translations, not only confusion but delusion is the consequence.

B

In his book *Gnosiology,* Kotarbinski asserts the principle that scientific advances have always emerged from the study of things with the implied, and frequently stated, presumption that any other course is the road to delusion. Among those psychologists whom I would include as proponents of a Reistic view in addition to Watson are E. R. Guthrie, Clark L. Hull, Edward C. Tolman, B. F. Skinner, and Donald Hebb, as well as their students—prominent among whom are O. Hobart Mowrer, Neal E. Miller, and Charles E. Osgood. This is indeed an imposing list —each has been a President of the American Psychological Association. Not every one mentioned would immediately and whole-heartedly endorse Reism without some qualification, to be sure, nor are they always consistent, but the net impact of their work has been Reistic, that is, a commitment to working with things in motion.

The fact that objectively oriented psychologists are preoccupied with things in motion makes them unreceptive to the concepts that concern laymen or even scientists in other areas, who, when they venture beyond their own boundaries of expertise, engage in rhetoric which purports to communicate but rarely does. To talk in terms of the will and morality, values, guilt, the goals of society or the national conscience is so much empty phraseology. The turmoil on some of our campuses echoes with the rhetoric of revolution, with cries of 'power to the people' and similar noises which are bereft of meaning. On all sides I hear expressions demanding that *Universities* must change but rarely do I hear *from what* and *to what* the changes should be. No one has yet stated the goals of universities in any terms other than pious platitudes which are never examined, possibly for fear that like the Emperor's new clothes they might be found quite unreal.

It is when we try to make contact with the world of values and morality that the separation or gulf between the science of human behavior and common thought and practice is most sharply revealed. The efforts of man to structure his society and to run it by the rule of law based on non-scientific assumptions of the lawmakers about the nature of man have been met by little in the way of success. In our nation's capitol the lawmakers are afraid to walk the streets and the situation is little better in the rest of our country. Our social problems, instead of decreasing with our growing productivity and technology, are increasing. Our efforts of amelioration consist again of rhetoric, more laws in some cases, and the elimination of some laws in other cases where crime is reduced because certain behaviors are no longer considered crimes.

Besides the rhetorical gambit of reducing crime by legalizing formerly illegal behavior (*e.g.* abortions), we have allowed our society to tolerate or nourish crime by denying the criminality of the perpetrator. Every day judges dismiss criminals because they are young or old, sick, alcoholic, under the influence of other drugs, first offenders, feeble-minded or insane, or because they were not properly charged, informed of their rights, or the evidence was not properly obtained. Our citizens cherish our Founding Fathers and the Constitution they developed, but half the population would not approve of the Bill of Rights if they were not first informed that they were being questioned about that Bill. People fight for a faith they do not understand or even question.

The contrast between our successes in dealing with things, witness our great technological successes, and our failure in dealing with social problems points up the unreistic operations by which we attempt to solve our social problems. With most of our social problems we avoid reality. In this state we pass abortion laws for women over 21 when the major problem is with unwed teen-agers. The problems of unwed mothers, like those of drugs and criminality, we attack with rhetoric.

I am by no means necessarily opposed to the actions of judges who dismiss criminals for one or another reason. What I want to point up is that there has come about in our society a situation where frequently it is not the criminal who is on trial, but, rather, someone is accusing society itself of creating the circumstances where crime becomes somehow inevitable. Thus there is a growing sense that something is wrong with our value system and, among other things, I suggest that part of what is wrong is that to a considerable extent our value system has been based on rhetoric, by which I mean words empty of meaning.

I shall try to suggest how such empty expressions or 'onamatoids' (Kotarbinksi's term) referring to non-things, or 'apparent things' can and do get us into trouble. I ask your indulgence in considering first, and primarily for illustrative purposes, the general area of accidents after which I will conclude with some tentative observations about the general area of right and wrong.

We have become so accustomed to dealing with labels and linguistic fictions that our base for launching attacks on important and costly problems such as develop from accidents is seriously undermined. During World War II, I was involved in accident prevention in aviation training programs. At that time I had a difficult task convincing my superiors that there was no such thing as an accident. That was difficult enough, but it was even more difficult to convince anyone that accidents could not be caused by carelessness (the universal explanation) because there was no such thing as 'carelessness.' I tried my best to explain that a given 'accident' did not happen by chance or through the operation of some immaterial agency like 'stupidity,' but had to happen in the precise way that it did because of specific behaviors that had occurred.

One particular type of behavior (landing airplanes without lowering the wheels) gave me my opportunity. I was able to show (Bugelski, 1945) that those so-called accidents were quite specifically programmed into the student fliers by their instructors. At my particular base of operations, students were trained to fly a particular route to the home field. About five miles from the field, if they were on course, they would cross over a bridge. At this point (a definite and specific marker, signal, or cue) they were instructed to lower their wheels so that when they arrived at the field they could feel free to attend to several other tasks required for landing. Day after day they did so. When some un-anticipated event such as a failure of a gas pump, a radio breakdown, bad weather, or other occasion required that they fly home in some more direct manner than circling out toward the bridge, they arrived at the field with wheels up and promptly proceeded to land that way. The regular and standard official judgment was: Pilot Error, 100%. Carelessness, 100%. Even the student pilots asserted that they were stupid, careless, lacking in foresight, faulty in memory, *etc.*

In the course of my actions I managed to change the operation to eliminate the over-the-bridge routine with a new instruction to lower wheels when circling the field at a point $90°$ to the landing runway. There were no more wheels-up landings. Not a word had been said about carelessness. No one was asked to be more careful. That would have been, as it is today, a waste of breath.

I come down to the conclusion, then, that there can be no science of psychology or behavior if we persist in studying the unstudiable. If we persist in talking about minds, wills, consciences, personalities, traits, intelligence, and the whole armamentarium of the mentalist we not only do not communicate, we obfuscate. To take the other course is so diffi-cult a choice as to frighten us. We have all been programmed so strongly with an arsenal of powerful but meaningless words and have used them so much with high degrees of success or personal satisfaction that we can hardly dream of altering them, or, worse still, disposing of them. We cherish our words and think we communicate when we talk as if we were transmitting meanings through the air in our conversations (a view that the anthropologist, Malinowski, 1938, once labeled the 'basket-theory' of meaning) when all we are doing is tapping into the programs of our listeners, setting off reactions of a largely emotional nature in them. To the extent that our programs are the same or similar, we may be communicating. To the extent that they differ, we are in trouble. Consider the impact of a phrase like 'flesh color' on a Negro; or better still, consider the impact on various audiences of such words as 'we must follow a democratic process.' The range of reactions to such a statement can run from strong agreement to violent disagreement depending upon the issues involved, as well as the nature of the speaker and his audience.

An almost insurmountable difficulty arises from our having been so thoroughly enraptured and confused with words. We can not make progress without talking, but talking the way we do leads to *no* progress. We can hardly glimpse a way out of our dilemma. Maybe the way out is to use only words that refer to things, to concrete objects, static or in motion, with very specific denotations.

The behaviorist view argues that just as knowledge and skills are programmed by experience, so is so-called morality and so-called decision-making. In short, the decision (actually, a person responding in a certain way) about to be made in any context or situation, has already been made, determined, programmed, and any subsequent reports of spiritual conflict, choice, or responsibility are quite irrelevant. Whether a decision is viewed as good or bad, right or wrong is a response of the external observer as a function of his programming; for the decision-maker it is always good and right at the time of decision even though subsequent events may lead the maker to say 'I was wrong.'

To appreciate the programming procedure involved we can examine a sample of nefarious behavior. Consider a purse-snatcher. He sees an accessible purse and this stimulus activates an emotional response we loosely call a desire. The purse signifies money and money is good. The fact that it is someone else's money is irrelevant to a purse-snatcher. He had not been programmed effectively to react to that feature of a situation. You might say he has not developed a conscience or a strong Super-Ego. That could be correct only if you view a conscience as some kind of reaction pattern that includes a sanction against theft. He might very well have a conscience or reaction pattern that places thievery among the routine or even admirable features of appropriate or good behavior. Who will argue that the Mafia does not possess a moral code which calls for obedience, loyalty, complete trust and honesty within the brotherhood?

The high probability exists that the purse snatcher with some successful background in the field never stops to consider the moral question. He may look about for police whom he has been programmed to regard as the enemy (the forces of Evil) but that is about all that might give him pause. From a behaviorist's view the purse-snatcher deserves no blame. He is behaving as he could be expected to. When he goes to court the judge worries over his 'responsibility' because our laws are all based on the assumption that our citizens are responsible for their acts. These laws were phrased by irresponsible lawyers, not psychologists who quite generally assume that no one is responsible for his behavior. That behavior is a product of his programming whether by nature or experience.

Now, let us look at the other side of the picture. Consider someone who finds a lost wallet, examines it, notes an identification card with an address and returns the wallet or drops it into a mail-box without even examining it for money. Such a paragon of Presbyterian programming deserves no credit. His honesty is no credit to him as he is equally helpless to the purse-snatcher. He happens to have been programmed differently. He deserves no praise.

We can now face the somewhat more complex problem where the purse-snatcher or the wallet-finder hesitates—he is in conflict, momentary or extended. What can we say of those tormented souls? The programming has not been effective, efficient, or complete. The individual is torn, we say, when we mean stimulated to do two contradictory things, to approach and avoid. A human can and does talk to himself. He begins to label his tendencies—'that's the right thing to do'—or—'that's the wrong thing to do.' Without knowing his programmers we can not tell what the 'that' is that is referred to. Sooner or later one conditioned stimulus gains the momentary ascendancy and he does one thing or the other. He will have done the right thing and the wrong thing at the same time, depending on the viewpoint of viewers. No one ever does the wrong thing from his own point of view.

From a behaviorist position the problem of ethics or morals in terms of absolutes or categorical imperatives vanishes into a nothingness. This is not to say that behaviorists espouse or endorse either immorality or amorality. They too have been programmed and they approve or disapprove of behavior in accordance with their own programming. Because most of them are middle-class, educated, peaceful citizens, they regard thievery as undesirable behavior which should be eliminated. Such elimination can be achieved by prisons, eliminating the need for money, or by reprogramming. The first of these steps is relatively easy. The second probably impossible, and the third, usually called rehabilitation, is exceedingly difficult given our present social structure.

The brief excursion into morality illustrates the principles of a reistic, behavioristic approach. A term like 'crime' or 'sin' does not refer to any thing in itself. There are no crimes. They cannot be observed, measured, or studied. Only behavior can be studied and that only in terms of people and movements. Drinking alcoholic beverages is behavior. Before 1918 it was not a crime. After 1918 and until 1932 it was. After 1932 it was not. The behaviour was practiced throughout the period with some alterations depending upon the label then in vogue. Today smoking marijuana is a crime. Currently the Congress and various state legislatures are considering the social problems involved and there are efforts to eliminate the criminal label. In a few years marijuana smoking may not be a crime. The smoking of the substance will probably continue.

In my own recent work I have begun to re-examine the role of imagery in learning and meaning. I have tried to avoid the error of reification and have no desire to restore the image to the catalogue of scientific observables, even potentially as some kind of hypothetical construct. When I speak of imagery I mean only that when people are asked to imagine something they report that they can do so quite easily in most cases. What goes on inside them I do not know, although I seriously doubt they develop and examine static pictures in their minds. I presume, instead, that some neurological reaction is generated by words or other stimuli (or other neurological actions) that are similar to the neurological reactions undergone at some earlier time when some other physical stimuli were impinging upon them. Through conditioning words have now come to replace such stimuli, in part, but only in part. Happily for my purposes, the subjects can apparently talk about these verbally generated reactions in words they might use in talking about the original stimuli.

When I (Bugelski, 1971) ask people to describe their reactions to words read to them one at a time I find that the viewpoint I have been describing receives considerable support. In my research I ordinarily read a list of some so-called concrete words (*e.g.* dog, table) and some so-called abstract words (*e.g.* love, peace, communism). Some words might fall into either group (*e.g.* flower, animal, furniture); these I call 'category' words.

When the subjects describe their reactions it does not matter what kind of word I use, the reactions generally are quite concrete. The word 'dog' for example calls out a reaction involving some specific, individual dog, a particular animal in a specific posture. This same reaction might be elicited by the word 'animal.' The word 'flower' evokes responses in terms of 'a rose' or 'a daisy' and again the rose is red or white, a single blossom or a bush, and so on. The word 'communism' was described by one girl as eliciting a response of 'a red velvet wall with a yellow hammer and sickle.' The word 'love' evokes alleged images of a specific sex partner; 'justice' is, for some, a blind goddess; for others, a black-robed figure, a courtroom, or even a television performer.

What I find, as did Bishop Berkeley in the 17th century, is that people think quite specifically, quite concretely, quite denotatively, and quite idiosyncratically when they are thinking, but they talk quite generally, abstractly, connotatively when they are talking, and since, in my view they are talking about what they are thinking about, they do not communicate. I think the message is quite clear for us. To learn about the human mind, if that is how we want to characterize behavior, and about values, we must return to a concern with specifics, to the observation and study of concrete things in motion and free ourselves from words that function as deluders and misleaders in our discussions. By persisting in the use of non-reistic language, we hardly improve our appreciation of behavioral problems, individual and social. We, instead, enfeeble ourselves while the problems grow in intensity and immensity.

Body, Mind, and Values

LUDWIG VON BERTALANFFY

State University of New York at Buffalo

I

I have been asked to talk about the problem of the relation between body, mind and values. Obviously this is a question philosophers have discussed for some 2,500 years: you can hardly expect me to give a final answer. Nevertheless, any period has to take a stand in regard to the perennial problems of philosophy, in terms of its own lights—that is, in terms of its scientific knowledge, epistemology, and world-outlook in general.

The point of departure for consideration of the mind-body problem is, obviously, the well known Cartesian dualism. Apparently, we find in our immediate experience two opposing parts or portions. On the one hand, there is the experience of things around us; tables and mountains and people and other organisms, stars seen in the telescope, cells observed in the microscope, and so forth. This 'objective' experience is said to be public; that is, it is shared by any observer who is placed in the right time and space coordinates. This consistitutes the *res extensa* of Descartes, the world of things extended in space. On the other hand, when I close my eyes and exclude outer or perceptual experience, there remains another part, the 'subjective.' I experience myself, for example, as carrying through certain processes of thought; further there are emotions, volitions and the rest. This, then, is the world of mind or consciousness, and this experience is said to be 'private.' It is not shared by other beings; 'thought,' 'emotions,' *etc.*, are in my consciousness alone. You can check that there are chairs around, and everybody else can see them too; similarly, you can check the pointer readings which lead to the conceptions of atoms or of nucleic acids; but the outside observer, by and large, is not in the position to tell whether just now I am thinking of Brahms' first symphony or of my income tax return. This is the private world, and according to its outstanding characteristic, Descartes called it the *res cogitans,* the 'thinking' or 'conscious' entity.

From this immediate experience we come to the representation of experience in concepts which in its elaborate form is called 'science.' In this conceptual representation the world of the spatial senses becomes a substance called matter. In the conception of classical materialism, and also of Descartes himself, matter consists of ultimate entities called atoms, that is little elastic billiard balls following the Newtonian laws of mechanics. This is one model which can, however, be refined in the progress of science. Thus the mechanically conceived atoms of classical physics were replaced by the elementary particles of modern physics: protons, electrons, neutrons, in sum, a few hundred kinds of elementary particles that obey laws of a more complex nature which are different from the familiar laws of macrophysics. Nevertheless, the basic conception regarding the objective part of experience remains. On the other side, we have a conceptual representation of 'inner' experience. As with respect to 'outer' experience, we are left with a concept of substance called 'matter,' so we also seem to have in the realm of 'inner' experience, something persisting or substantial, which is called 'mind' or 'psyche.' My experience shows a continuity when I go to sleep and wake up again; my ego, self or whatever you call it, persists in time by means of phenomena like memory which connects the past and the present. In a similar way as the conception of matter is introduced to account for persistency in the things of outside experience in perception, a corresponding persistent entity or substance, mind, is introduced for persistencies in the realm of inner or subjective experience.

We have, therefore, to distinguish these two levels: the level of *immediate experience,* and that of *conceptual constructs* or models, which finds its sophisticated expression in sciences or rather in sciences like physics on the one hand and psychology on the other, both terms taken in a broad sense.

As we know, the problem of the relations of matter and mind was kicked around by philosophers over the centuries and there have been numerous attempts to bring these two halves of experience, these two worlds or two substances, into some intelligible relation by theories known as materialism, idealism, psychophysical interaction, parallelism or identity, phenomenalism and others. We cannot say that these attemps were particularly successful; rather, the struggle between these theories consisted essentially in their mutual refutation. One can nicely show that, for well-defined reasons, the theory of psychophysical interaction is unsatisfactory; but then, the theory of psychophysical parallelism was not better, and so down the list. Hence the history of the problem is essentially the mutual refutation of competing theories.

On top of this we have the realm of values which again remains highly dubious. In some way or other, values are often supposed to be reducible either to matter or to mind. In the first sense, it is easy to see that certain values arise from the material or biological organism of man. In this sense values like the pleasure principle or the principle of self-maintenance are based on biological principles; similarly certain social values may be reduced to the preservation of the species as is expressed already in altruistic instincts of social animals. But on the other hand, values tend to be considered products of the mind; they appear to be ideas with certain emotional emphasis expressed as the good, the beautiful and the true.

This is the simplest presentation I am able to give of the traditional problem of body, mind and values. Philosophers, of course, have expressed it in a hundred more sophisticated ways; but more or less it amounts to what I have said, in terms of traditional epistemology and metaphysics.

Now, however, it seems to me, the time has come to revise these traditional concepts; not so much by way of adding new hypotheses to the old ones I mentioned, such as those of parallelism, interaction, epiphenomenalism and so forth, but rather by way of an inspection and revision of the very bases of the traditional concepts. There are a number of reasons to do so, a review of which would require more time than I have available. One of the more obvious reasons lies in the fact that the traditional concepts of matter and mind do not suffice any more in view of modern developments in science, or rather in quite a number of sciences ranging from physics and biology to psychology, psychopathology and culturology, to linguistics and others.

II

In this brief outline we must bring things to the simplest possible framework. In this sense I remind you of a rather obvious consideration. As is well-known, matter, as it was sometimes said, has 'dematerialized' in modern physics; the ultimate entities of physics cannot be described anymore with concepts that stem from an early time of physics in the

16th–17th century when rather primitive notions such as atoms conceived as little billiard balls seemed to suffice. This can be seen easily in the fact that the physics of elementary particles in modern times has become identical with high-energy physics, as is expressed in the famous Einstein formula. This implies what I have already intimated; namely, there are no minute entities any more with characteristics taken from everyday observation, that is, hard little bodies, impenetrable, elastic, and so forth. Rather, matter appears as a sort of nodal point in a highly abstract and unvisualizable 'substance' which we call energy, and of which nothing can be predicated except that it is defined by certain mathematical relations and that its behavior is describable by similarly abstract and unvisualizable mathematical relationships or laws. In the last resort, one may say, the only persistent entities or substances according to modern physics are certain invariances of extremely abstract mathematical concepts, such as conservation of energy of spin, parity and the like—entities that are quite unvisualizable and can only be described by rather difficult, mathematical expressions. This is about all that is left of matter in the sense of everyday observation and of classical science.

In a similar way, the concept of mind as Descartes and other philosophers had it, is not sufficient anymore in psychological science. The concept of mind was reasonably well-defined so long as mind could be identified with consciousness; and this is actually expressed in Descartes' concept of the *res cogitans*. But just as in physics the popular notion of matter has dissolved, as it were, and had to be replaced by much more abstract notions, something similar happened also in psychology; even though, of course, we are aware that physics is a 'hard' science, while psychology in our days is a very weak science. Nevertheless here, too, a conceptual framework has to be introduced for explanation of phenomena; but it remains unvisualizable or unexperienceable. We all speak of the unconscious and find this notion necessary to explain many psychological phenomena. But the concept of the unconscious violates the very definition of mind which was based on the characteristic of conscious experience. The unconscious is a conceptual construct introduced to explain certain observable phenomena in 'inner' experience, just as the abstract constructs of physics were introduced to explain certain phenomena in outer experience.

So the Cartesian dualism and its two basic concepts, matter and mind, look rather shadowy indeed, and little is left of classical dualism. If I had more time, I would have to elaborate in more detail that the world of science is the world of our conceptual constructs. On the other hand, I would have to elaborate that looking at things phenomenologically, that is, going back to direct or immediate experience, the apparent basic dualism (things outside; I myself in-side) is not a primary datum that can be used as self-evident basis of metaphysics. Rather it is the product of a long development in child psychology and of a long evolution in the history and culture of man-kind. The dualism apparent in our experience is nothing absolute but is based on conceptualizations characteristic of mature, Western man. The experienced worlds of the child, the primitive, probably even the Indian or Chinese, are quite different from ours.

This would require a much more detailed examination. In the present compass, I can only state that the concept of values also takes on a dif-ferent meaning. As already said, we have on the one side what may be termed biological values, that is values that arise from biological exis-tence, and are a verbalization and partly a sublimation of biological 'givens.' As there is a tendency of the living organism to maintain itself, it is natural that the principle of self-preservation, the pleasure principle and similar ones belong to the 'biological' values. This is also true of many social values; it is well to remember that man is a social animal and that many animals are even better equipped with social instincts. In a beehive or ant hill there is no social problem, no revolutions, no strife between generations and races, for the excellent reason that social 'values' in bees and ants are instinctive and inborn. Moral principles such as the Golden Rule and similar precepts certainly have their roots in, and are verbalizations of social instincts. Without these, man could not even have started his evolution, history and culture.

On the other hand, however, there are many values which are ap-parently *not* of a biological nature. One may call them specifically 'human' values. We find that besides those social values which man shares with social animals, there are many which are unbiological, have no biological meaning in terms of the preservation of the individual, society and species, and may even contradict and destroy the latter.

I do not think that it can be maintained in any way that—say—Peri-clean architecture, sculpture and tragedy was biologically or socially useful; indeed this Athenian culture and society soon had a catastrophic end. The same is true of Renaissance painting or German music and innumerable other 'cultural' values, and—yes—even of science. Science is eminently practical because we can apply it in technology. Trivially, social progress in the last few centuries has proved the biological-social value of science; but we have not seen the end and have still to learn

whether science is a highway to utopia or a *cul-de-sac* with atomic fireworks at its end.

In an early novel by Aldous Huxley, a remarkable conversation is
reported between the lover (who happens to be an intellectual and a
snob) and his girl friend. In Rome's Villa Giulia (the well-known
Etruscan museum) she desperately asks: 'What have those—bloody—
Etruscans to do with me—with my personal concerns, worries and life?'
His answer: 'Absolutely nothing. For that's the definition of culture—
knowing and thinking about things that have absolutely nothing to do
with us. About Etruscans, for example, or cat's cradle among the
Chinese, or the Universe at large.' One may also remember what
Cannon—creator of the concept of homeostasis—said about the pre-
cious unessentials—that is, all that is beyond homeostasis, equilibrium,
adaptation—and without which, nevertheless, there would be neither
life nor culture.

As you cannot fashion a biological theory of value that includes those
specifically human values, so you cannot give a psychological theory, for
the reason that the universe of values far transcends the psychology of
their makers. This is what many ethical and all religious systems claim,
namely, that ethical values transcend the interests of the individual and
of society. Take the biblical command, 'Love thy neighbor as thyself.'
Obviously, the maxim has never been followed; and if it would be followed—say, in the ways of Saint Francis of Assisi—it would be destructive of society as it actually exists. So we do not find a foundation
for many human values in terms of social utilitarianism; and equally
human values and value systems transcend psychology.

It rather appears that the universe of values is part of a certain world
beyond the universes of physics and biology; we may call this third the
symbolic universe. It is the universe of symbolic activities and their
conceptual and material realizations created by man and, so far as we
know, created only by man and by no other beings. It transcends man
as a biological, psychological and social entity, and follows its own
immanent laws. This is clearly the status of language, science, art and
other symbolic universes. Take, for example, language, and note that
its laws and developments are not psychological laws. A simple illustration is Grimm's law of consonant changes stating that in the evolution of Indo-germanic languages there is a lawful sequence of
consonants like t, th, d, which has taken place generally. But
this certainly is not a psychological law. This particular example is
taken from phonetics; but essentially the same applies to grammar, and
to cultural developments in general. We may correctly say that music

from Palestrina to Beethoven, Wagner and Strauss followed well-definable laws—but these are not psychological laws concerning the individual composers. The same holds true for the history of any 'cultural' realm. Thus the whole realm of symbolic worlds, be it of art, science, politics or what have you, has its own autonomous principles and laws; and so also have those aspects of symbolism which are called values.

This is the reason why not only a 'biologistic' ethics (hedonism, preservation of the species, *etc.* as supreme values) but also an ethics of 'self-realization' does not correspond to the 'human fact', that is, the actuality of human behavior and history. Ethics is understood here as being a description relating 'what humans actually do,' not a normative stipulation as to 'what they ought to do.' Even so, it is obvious that realization of what appears to be specifically human, is more than 'self-realization' of the human individual, its wishes, urges, potentialities, *etc.* Rather it is 'self-transcendence,' that is, realization of values going beyond the individual, or realization (in the terminology here applied) of 'symbolic' universes. This is the definition of every culture, from the most primitive taboos to the highest flights of art, science and mystical religion. Obeying even the most primitive and strange taboos of some wild tribe transcends self-realization (and indeed often consists of most painful and self-abnegating procedures which are opposite to the individual's wishes, pleasure and well-being) as well as what is useful for the group's, tribe's or species' benefit. In the same way, the highest manifestations of culture are (and always have been) 'self-transcendent.' It can hardly be seen that Michelangelo contributed to the 'standard of living' of his contemporaries and of subsequent generations, and if his work was self-realization of his potentials, the psychological price paid was excessive in terms of a 'healthy' or 'well-adjusted personality.' Again, the overthrow of the Ptolemaic world picture and the foundation of Newtonian physics was a purely 'spiritual' exercise, that is, neither born from economic factors nor contributing to individual self-realization or social 'progress.' Technological exploitation of science came centuries later, and we still do not know whether the result is 'the greatest happiness of the greatest number,' whether, in balance, it diminished or increased human misery. Martyrs—from Socrates to early Christians or Giordano Bruno—did change history, but their self-realization rather was self-destruction, and whether they contributed to 'progress' in the sense of better plumbing, improved health and more automobiles, remains highly dubious.

In this sense, 'specifically human' or 'cultural' values are 'self-transcendent,' that is, go far beyond the benefit of the individual or the species; and do this not in the way of a supernatural precept or command, but as a mere descriptive fact, in terms of what actually happened in human individuals and in history.

Thus we have essentially three universes; of nonliving things, of living nature, and of symbolic entities. If I am speaking of three universes, I do not mean of course that they are unconnected with one another. Being a biologist, I should be aware that there are transitions between non-living things and living things; similarly, it would be easy to show that there are transitions and preparatory stages between biological and social phenomena on the one hand and the symbolic worlds of culture on the other. By and large, however, it will be correct to say that the principle of emergence applies, which means that a higher level cannot be simply reduced to, or built up from, the proximate lower level. Rather, each level has an existence of its own and its own laws. For example, the laws in biology are not simply the laws of inanimate nature we know in physics, for new aspects appear such as the order of processes and self-maintenance we find in living systems, the genetic code and many other features that are not encountered in nonliving objects. Similarly, as I have emphasized, the laws prevailing in a symbolic universe are not psychological laws.

To give one further example, consider the laws of algorithms as, for example, that of multiplication or the procedures of higher mathematics. If you perform a simple multiplication using decimal notation, you employ an algorithm; and so you do in any other, more sophisticated exercise of logic and mathematics. But this algorithm is not reducible to psychological principles of conditioning, learning theory, the unconscious, and the like; it is a structure within a system of symbols.

In summary: what we call values, are partly verbalizations or symbolizations of biological 'givens,' and this applies to many egotistic and societal values in behavior. But some values transcend those biological universes; these are the so-called higher values, which are frequently biologically useless or even opposed to biological values, as is dramatically the case with the suicide and the martyr. The suicide is a case where the very biological system is destroyed under pressure of certain values (that is, symbolic systems) because the suicide does not fit into and actually protests the prevailing, socio-cultural system. Similarly, the martyr for an idea acts against those utilitarian rules which serve the maintenance of the individual and of society. The Christian martyrs did not go into the arena to be eaten by wild beasts because they wanted to improve the social conditions in the Roman Empire;

they let themselves be destroyed because of their faith—that is, because of their unshakeable adherence to certain symbolic structures, a certain construction of their universe.

Stating those three main levels (with any number of intermediates) of the physical, organismic and symbolic universes is, of course, far from being original. It is another expression of a 'given,' which was formulated in many different ways. The old distinction of body, mind and spirit hints in the same direction; so does the biblical and mystical trinity of the Father, Son and Holy Ghost. Again, there is Hegel's objective, subjective, and absolute spirit, or more recently Teilhard de Chardin's so-called lithosphere, biosphere and noosphere. These different expressions have, of course, different emphases, but they relate to the same 'given' that we seem to find in our exeprience: three levels or universes of the non-living, living, and symbolic.

From what I have said it immediately follows that among values some are very general and concern all human beings irrespective of race, creed and color; that is, these are values based upon biological preconditions which apply to the species 'man' in general. On the other hand, we find idiosyncratic values characteristic of specific sociocultural systems, of civilizations, societies, groups or individuals. In other words, the symbolic and value universes created by different cultures, societies, and ultimately different individuals, are very different: one man's meat is the other's poison. Man has invented the strangest totems and taboos and we know from history and anthropology that he is often more willing to fight, or to sacrifice himself, for these, than for his individual benefit, or the enlightened self-interest of his group, nation and so forth.

III

As we all know, there is a prevailing tendency in contemporary science and philosophy which is called reductionism, meaning that an attempt is made to reduce more complex phenomena and levels to simpler and lower ones. In this sense, sociology should be reduced to psychology, psychology to physiology, biology to physics, and eventually everything should be deducible in an all-encompassing mathematical system.

We cannot discuss the question of reductionism in its general, scientific and philosophical framework. However, it also applies to the problem of values with which we are concerned, and is here of particular relevance for the urgent problems of our time.

According to its basic thesis, the tendency of reductionism is to explain the human sector by subhuman entities, roughly speaking, by the behavior and psychology of non-human, animal species. It is interesting to see how this has found different expressions.

Among reductionist theories, the first was psychoanalysis. Although this does not do any justice to psychoanalytic theory, it can be stated that an essential tenet was the reduction of human behavior to so-called biological drives, sometimes called 'tissue needs' (that is, to the biological level) which tend to restore a psychological 'equilibrium' after disturbances. We have already noted, in passing, that many activities of human beings (and even of animals) by far transcend the scheme of 'homeostasis,' establishment of 'equilibrium' or self-maintenance.

Next came behaviorism or experimental psychology which was essentially an attempt to reduce human behavior to animal behavior—by and large, the behavior of the white laboratory rat in a Skinner box or some other conditioning device. In order to understand human behavior, we should apply the laws of operant conditioning and learning theory as derived from animal experimentation. Conversely, principles of behaviorism are applied in the control and engineering of human behavior; propaganda techniques from television commercials of cars and detergents to the 'Selling of the President,' are based upon conditioning techniques derived from behavioristic psychology. We have discussed this phenomenon elsewhere (1968) and in a short phrase, have called it 'The Return to the Conditioned Reflex,' in contrast to the human and civilized art of decision at a symbolic and meaningful level.

Again, more recent and presently much in vogue is the employment, for a similar purpose, of ethology or comparative study of behavior. Many similarities and parallelism are found between animal and human behaviors. This should not come as a surprise. Man being a mammal in his anatomy, physiology, biochemistry and so forth, it would be rather miraculous if the same would not be true of much of his instinctual and behavioral equipment. Comparative study—particularly of sexual and aggressive behavior—sheds much light on many aspects of human behavior. But Konrad Lorenz himself, founder of ethology, has emphasized that, in contrast to man considered as the 'Naked Ape,' something completely new came into the world with culture, cumulative tradition, language, *etc.* Hence abolition of cultural tradition—as aimed at by some revolutionary youth—would not make man into a Noble Savage living in a paradise but be a backslide of 200,000 years of human evolution.

Such wise reticence is alien to recent bestsellers. Man, then, is 'nothing but' a 'Naked Ape'; the war in Vietnam or the landing on the moon an expression of his 'Territorial Imperative'; the alleged suppression of woman in Western civilization a consequence of male 'bonding' supposedly (but not empirically) found in man's anthropoid ancestors and so on.

Many of the 'reductionist' claims can easily be shown to be unbridled speculations without foundation in ethological study but catering to a current fashion. More interesting is the consideration of 'reductionism' and the 'zoomorphic' conception of man as a symptom of the present *zeitgeist*. Man in this period of hyper-sophisticated technology, at the same time seems to take a masochistic pleasure in seeing himself as 'nothing but' a bundle of animal drives, an overgrown Skinner rat, an angry ape, a computer—indeed almost any biological or technological simile—excepting the mature, human person.

I cannot resist quoting the most amusing critique of recent ethology I encountered. It appeared in *The New Yorker* and was prefaced as being the author's (Ellis, 1968) 'last-ditch attempt to differentiate himself from a ten-spined stickleback':

> When naturalists grew tired of shooting and stuffing the creatures they loved . . . (they) began peering at them in the wild state . . . Soon there was scarcely a bird, an ape, a gazelle, a dragonfly whose bowings and scrapings, preening, threats, empurplings, and sac-swellings were not being observed somewhere by somebody. Amid the welter of head-noddings and twig-fiddlings thus brought to light, it was natural that certain resemblances between animal and human behavior should be noted . . . It had not at this state been suggested that because Horace Walpole decorated Strawberry Hill with colorful Gothic bric-a-brac he was practically indistinguishable from a bower-bird. The differences between man and beast were at first apparent even to the animal-behavior observers, or ethologists, who were at pains to remind their readers that animals were not human. 'Let us have none of this anthropomorphism!' . . . As recently as 1953, Tinbergen was writing 'It is scarcely necessary to stress the differences in type of organization between human societies and those of gulls.'
> It is highly necessary now. Scarcely had these ethologists finished shaking their fingers at sentimentalists who spoke of animals as though they were men when they themselves set to work to prove that men were animals. . . .

After narrating how, following the ethologists' example, Mr. Ellis set up a tent in Hyde Park for studying the behavior of the human animals, and encountered a London bobby's wrath, he concludes:

> He (the policeman) turned so extraordinary a color around the neck
> that a less objective observer might have supposed he was ready to
> mate. But I have been long enough at the game to recognize aggres-
> sion when I see it, whether in stickleback or man. We now had an
> almost perfect setup for a demonstration of the territorial imperative.
> The blind was my territory, and so long as I was in it I *must* be the
> dominant individual. The policeman, however, had pretty obviously
> never read Mr. Ardrey, so I took to my heels. This proves, I think,
> that I am less of a chacma baboon than some other enthologists I
> could name. (Ellis, 1968).

Quite recently, reductionism has found still another, particularly para-
doxical form. As a reaction against the 'robot model' of man in behaviorism (trying, as mentioned, to reduce human behavior and
psychology to the principles of rat psychology, particularly operant
conditioning, secondary reinforcement and learning theory) a 'humanistic' psychology was proposed, often considered and denominated as
the 'third force' in contrast to psychoanalysis and behaviorism. Obviously, such psychology should emphasize and explore what is specifically 'human' in man's behavior, and there is a dire need for it. If—
as ethology makes abundantly clear—there are specific differences (to
be investigated in each individual case) between the behaviors of different species of geese or coral fish, it is hardly a bold assumption that
somewhat greater differences will prevail between the laboratory rat and
the species named (with some exaggeration) *Homo sapiens*. It is therefore quite in the line of ethological thinking to investigate these differences; and instead of introducing a new programmatic slogan, it
may be just as well simply to speak of 'human' as distinguished from
rat or stickleback behavior and psychology.

Important beginnings were made, for example, by the late A.
Maslow. His emphasis on normal as contrasted to pathological psychology, on self-realization of the human personality, his distinction between 'deficiency cognition' of everyday life, governed by utilitarian
principles and within the framework of long-conditioned categories, and
'being cognition' in 'peak experiences' breaking out from mere utilitarianism and inveterate symbolic frameworks and returning to the
freshness of primal experience, indeed emphasize aspects of human
nature suppressed and neglected in psychoanalytic, behavioristic and
ethological theories. Other efforts of the 'third force,' for example
Charlotte Bühler's elaboration of 'life's natural tendencies,' are important contributions toward 'human psychology' in the sense mentioned, as are the elaboration of the theory of symbolism as man's

distinctive feature, the exploration of developmental psychology in the work of Piaget and Heinz Werner and so forth.

But look what has happened. As S. Koch (1969)—author of the many-volume work, *Psychology—The Study of a Science*—recently wrote:

> . . . I caught up with the 'humanistic psychologists' last fall at the annual American Psychological Association meeting in San Francisco . . . The humanistic fervor of the group has been channeled into one activity, variously designated as group therapy, T-group therapy, sensitivity group therapy, syntectics, etc. I had known of the proliferation of forms of group therapy, but had not known that the whole energy of formal 'humanistic psychology" is now given to its pursuit . . . By far the largest audience showed up at a symposium in which Paul Bindrim, the originator of 'nude-marathon group therapy,' spoke and showed a film . . . Bindrim's methods, for the most part, are the standard devices of group therapy. He was enthusiastic at the symposium, however, about a therapeutic invention of his own inspired coinage that he calls 'crotch-eyeballing.' The crotch, he notes, is the focus of many hang-ups. In particular, three classes; (1) aftermath difficulties of toilet training; (2) masturbation guilts; (3) stresses of adult sexuality. Why not blast all this pathology at once! Thus two group members aid in (as Bindrim says) the 'spread-eagling' of a third member and the entire company is instructed to stare unrelentingly and for a good long interval at the offending target area. Each group member is given an opportunity to benefit from this refreshing psychic boost . . .

We are not here concerned with legitimate group therapy as a valuable tool of psychotherapy. Neither need we enter into discussion of the 'Human Potential Movement' which recently has been given a well-documented and witty survey (Howard, 1970). It is well understandable that in a society which is deprived of emotional and instinctual warmth in the sole pursuit of intellectual and economical ends, which has lost ancient arts such as conversation, flirt and sexual foreplay, which is exposed to a crushing monotony of life, is deradicated and lonely in a modern nomadism, depersonalized in the 'megamachine' of present society, denied personal distinction except in terms of dollars 'made' or 'one is worth'—it is understandable, I say, that under such conditions some surrogate or *ersatz* for societal and civilized values is sought for, and may be beneficial in the emotional and cultural starvation amidst economic opulence. However, this trend itself tends to become 'reductionist' and commercial.

'Humanistic psychology' introduced to overcome the devaluation of man in a mechanized commercial society, thus tends to reduce man (and females) to 'a pullulating mass, an undifferentiated and diffused region in a social space,' (again borrowing from Koch), and does so by way of behavioral engineering (directed, this time, not toward conditioning of individuals but to reducing the individual to its animal common denominator in the group). While 'humanistic psychology' and the 'third force' arose as a protest against a commercially engineered society, it became itself 'big business.' Growth centers, human potential development and the like offer personality or salvation in ways not different from commercials promising the plain office girl transmutation into a great seductress or *femme fatale* by application of a new, 'enriched' skin cream.

What is depressing and terrifying is the fact that supposedly 'scientific' or 'humanistic' insights are uniformly exploited for the engineering and often degradation of human nature. It matters little in this regard, whether the human being is considered and managed as a robot, a Naked Ape or part of a sort of psychological slime-mould called the group.

To summarize as unequivocally as possible: It is obvious, as Ardrey states in a new book, that humans share with higher animals three innate needs: for identity, the opposite of anonymity; for stimulation, the opposite of boredom; and for security, the opposite of anxiety. Affluence produces the bored society and, together with denial of identity in a leveling egalitarianism, this leads to the need for ever-increased stimulation, from sex to violence to war in such a 'cancerous world.' This, in a vicious circle, leads to the 'information overload' discussed by Tosser as another symptom of this sick time.

These, then, are 'drives' biological in their roots, manifest in a troop of monkeys, and starved in present conditions of overcrowding urbanization and individuality-murdering mechanization. However, in this human predicament or man's being 'thrown' not only into hostile nature but upon his own instinctual equipment, there were imposed, first, the reins of material wants, and secondly those of the superstructure of 'human' values, that is, those 'symbolic' universes in social relations, higher emotions, art, religion and so forth. Take them away, as is the case in the 'Decline of the West', of material abundance and emotional starvation; and there remains only uninhibited, destructive *bête humaine* made so infinitely more dangerous than any beast because of the brain or intelligence endowment of the human species. It is well that we recognize how delicate is the distinction separating man and beast; but just because of this we must not help to destroy it.

We may well agree that the one-sided dominion of intellect (of 'science and technology') implies an atrophy of the other, emotional aspects of human nature. In its fullness, 'culture' or the 'symbolic system' includes not only intellect but is also basic for all 'higher' emotions, therefore its decline is ensured by the 'reduction' or contemporary bestialization in sex, aggression and other respects. We cannot offer a remedy or miracle cure; we can only repeat that the preservation of 'values' in society, and preservation of that society itself, implies that symbolic superstructure which is fundamental for both human culture and human personality.

Notes and References

'APA Weighs Pros, Cons of Encounter Groups.' *Psychiatric News*, May 1970.

Ardrey, R. *The Territorial Imperative*. New York: Atheneum, 1966.

Ardrey, R. *The Social Contract*. Preprint in *Life*, September 11, 1970.

Bertalanffy, L. von. 'The Mind-body Problem: A New View', *Psychosomatic Medicine*, Vol. 24, 1964.

Bertalanffy, L. von. 'On the Definition of the Symbol.' In: J. R. Royce (ed.), *Psychology and the Symbol*. New York: Random House, 1965, pp. 127–72.

Bertalanffy, L. von. 'Mind and Body Re-Examined.' *Journal of Humanistic Psychology*, Fall 1966, pp. 113–38.

Bertalanffy, L. von. *Robots, Men and Minds*. New York: Braziller, 1969.

Bugenthal, James F. T. (ed.) *Challenges of Humanistic Psychology*. New York: McGraw-Hill, 1967.

Ellis, H. F. 'The Naked-Ape Crisis', *The New Yorker*, 1968.

Fried, M. H. Review of 'Man in Groups'. *Science* 165, 883–4, 1969.

Howard, Jane. *Please Touch*. New York: McGraw-Hill Book Co., 1970.

Huxley, Aldous. *After the Fireworks*. New York: Harper, 1929.

Koch, Sigmund. 'Stimulus/Response'. *Psychology Today*, September, 1969.

Koestler, Arthur. *The Ghost in the Machine*. New York: MacMillian, 1968.

Koestler, Arthur (ed.). *Beyond Reductionism*. London: Hutchinson, 1969.

Leibowitz, L. 'Desmond Morris is Wrong About Breasts, Buttocks, and Body Hair.' *Psychology Today*, February, 1970.

Lorenz, Konrad. 'Rats, Apes, Naked Apes, Kipling, Instincts, Guilt, The Generations and Instant Copulation.'—A Talk with Konrad Lorenz: *The New York Times Magazine*, July 5, 1970.

Matson, Floyd W. Review of 'Man in Groups.' *Psychology Today*, December 1969.

Morris, D. *The Naked Ape*. New York: McGraw-Hill, 1968.

Tiger, L. *Man in Groups*. New York: Random House, 1969.

Psychoanalysis and Values

JOSEPH WILDER, M. D.

Coler Memorial Hospital, New York City

In approaching my subject let me mention first certain self-imposed limitations and certain liberties I shall take. I shall limit myself to ethical values in the broadest sense and exclude esthetic and scientific values. I shall take the liberty in speaking of psychoanalysis not to confine myself to the classical Freudian school of psychoanalysis but to include the methods and ideas of the many variants and developments of the psychology of the subconscious which emerged in the wake of Freud's discoveries.

Let me present my main conclusions at the very beginning and justify them later. We all know that we are living in a time of rapid changes of many important values and value systems necessitated by rapid technological, scientific, social and economic developments; that as a result we are witnessing a confusing and dangerous psychological situation not only in the young generation but in general. I claim that only a deeper and broader psychoanalytic insight into the causes and consequences of our reactions, as far as they are relevant to these problems, promises help. This is an area of our subconscious mind which has not yet been satisfactorily studied by psychoanalysis.

Man as an animal is often presented simply as an organism responding to stimuli. This is an over-simplification. Animals and, in higher degree, man, have a double response to stimuli: 1) an immediate response which as far as the psyche is concerned follows the pain–pleasure principle; here values do not apply; and 2) a long-range response which consists in accepting frustration of pleasure and acceptance of pain; this response is still in the service of the pain–pleasure principle because its aim is a gain in pleasure and avoidance of pain in the future. It seems that in more primitive man this long-range, self-frustrating response is less developed, but it definitely exists. Think of the various taboos, self-mutilations, *etc.* It also exists in animals; think of hibernation, hoarding for winter, effects of training. It even exists in mindless organisms without a brain in the form of the many nervous or enzymatic negative feedback mechanisms. However, we know definitely that the ability for this aimed self-frustration depends on a number of known psychological factors: intelligence, will power, temperament, education, training, *etc.* The brilliant psychoanalyst–philosopher Paul Schilder[1] expressed the situation somewhat differently: our strivings always aim at values. These are of two kinds: a) of low order, attached to things; b) of higher order, pertaining to thing structures. In striving for the latter we aim at ordering our drives into structural unity. He does not mention the permanent conflict between these more concrete and more abstract strivings.

We mention all this only to stress that ethical values have nothing to do with the first, the primitive and immediate pain–pleasure principle. They belong to the self-frustrating, delaying pain–pleasure principle. This is to emphasize that, contrary to superficial appearances, they still serve the pain–pleasure principle. And even if we accept Freud's concept of super-ego (only partly identical with conscience) in constant conflict with ego and libido, the outcome of this conflict still follows the pain–pleasure principle. Of course, the reward for the momentary frustration of the pain–pleasure principle may be in the very near or in the very distant future (e.g. in heaven, in posterity, *etc.*)

Seen in this way the origin of values is to be sought in a more or less enlightened self interest. However, this explanation will not satisfy those who see human nature as basically altruistic (Rousseau, Kant) or who, like Alfred Adler[2] and others, believe in the existence of special 'social feelings' in man, or those cynics who like Karl Marx or Nietzsche believe that moral ideas are deeply implanted by the ruling classes or who hypothesize that the individual has somewhere in his mind a consciousness of being a small part of whole humanity's past and future.

The reasons for and the goals of this self-frustrating, pleasure-delaying process are expressed either directly in terms of our better self-interest, of foresight, or in terms of values. We can think: if you hit your neighbor, he will hit you; if you forgive him or sue him nothing bad will happen to you. Or we can think still further ahead in terms of *values,* symbols, positive or negative, of violence, law and order, charity, sin, self-control, humility, *etc.* Very often these values are parts of a whole value system, *e.g.* religion.

Once we have learned or created the symbols called values they achieve a certain independence and serve as stimuli for action or in-action (positive and negative values).

You realize that in these and the following remarks I am endeavoring to convey a one-sided *psychologistic* view of values.

Thus to almost every stimulus, external or internal, inclusive of intra-psychic stimuli, we respond with a conflict between the immediate pain–pleasure response and the delayed pain–pleasure response. The delayed pain–pleasure response is in most cases bolstered by the establishment of values. The outcome of this conflict will depend on the intensity of the impulse and the intensity, or better, importance of the value or values involved. The values involved will depend on circumstances. If a girl in the Orient immediately satisfies every desire for sweets, whether it comes from the sight of sweets or the thought of sweets there are only a few things which may occasionally inhibit her, like the thought of saving her money or saving some of the sweets for later, or the wish not to spoil her appetite for the next meal; the values involved are parsimony and superior hedonism. The thought of getting fat, on the other hand, even spurs her on because a fat girl has a better chance of finding a husband and matrimony is a very high value. A child does not yet have this conflict; he satisfies the immediate urge; the obstacles are not values but parents and that means: society in the shape of parents. As the child grows up a little the actual parents are not necessary, the thought of them is associated with sweets and internalized. The child is faced by the high-ranking value of obedience. It has—to follow Freud—formed a super-ego, a kind of conscience.

An American girl of today wants sweets; but the thought of gaining weight, of becoming fat is associated with the idea of not getting a husband. Matrimony is here too a high value and it will cause our girl to postpone or even give up the gratification of her impulse. The same girl visits a wealthy aunt whose money she might inherit some day and is proudly offered aunt's specially made cookies; here the value of pro-spective wealth may conquer the value of being thin and the girl can indulge her impulse to eat. A man loves sweets but he is a diabetic; the high value of health will suppress his impulse to eat sweets. Were he born before medicine discovered diabetes this conflict would not exist, and maybe today he can eat sugar if he takes a sugar reducing medicine.

From these simple examples you can see that our values are very dependent on our culture, history, geography, economics, science, technology, social conditions. The fact that we live in a time when all these conditions are rapidly changing makes the topic of this conference so urgent. We would need a lexicon of values in which the meaning, the rank order, the history and economics of every single value and value system should be thoroughly and objectively analyzed, including, last but not least, its *psychology*. Such planning would perhaps help us to project the future fate and development of specific values and help us make our choices and decisions less difficult.

We can no longer afford, in making value choices or in the formation of our value systems, to follow intuitions, emotions, the charisma of a preacher, the hangups of our parents or the skill of an advertising agency. We must try to apply our intelligence, knowledge and experience systematically. In other words, I submit that we must program ourselves, form our value systems scientifically, no matter how incomplete our science may be. We must attempt this in spite of John Dewey's cautious warning: 'It would be too optimistic to say that we have as yet enough knowledge of the scientific type to enable us to regulate our judgments of value very extensively.'[3]

However, here the most formidable obstacle arises. One of the most important conditions of scientific thinking is that it must be value-free. And this is very difficult, perhaps impossible. On second glance we can adopt a more practical formulation: the value called 'truth' must in science supersede all other considerations, and science through the centuries is getting progressively better in uncovering and debunking falsehoods. Scientific psychology is one example. One other difficulty is that values don't stand still while we examine them at length. The process of e-, re-, de-valuation, upgrading, creation of new or abolishment of old values is a continuous process and it seems to be going on with progressive acceleration even if some values live longer than others. A number of known factors contribute to this progressive turn-over of values. One is the progressive spread of information. One would be tempted sometimes to speak of 'information pollution' were ignorance not an even greater danger. One result of the confusion of values is that we talk so much about what the world *will* be and so little about what it *should* be. We talk much about survival and often forget that the most important instruments of survival are our value systems. How strong are the values which will cause us to postpone—hopefully and *ad infinitum*—the eating of that candy or the pressing of that atomic button?

It is not possible here to discuss such important subjects as specific values and their historical development; the enormous changes in values and value systems in the present era and their causes; the predictions for future developments; their manifestations in the present youth movements, *etc.* I am sure that you have all reflected about this quite a bit. There is a growing literature on the subject, although little based on scientific methods. I hope to comment on this elsewhere.

My thesis is that in order to better understand the present serious situation and devise better methods for dealing with the enormous problem of changing values we can no longer proceed in an intuitive and crudely experimental way. Freud in his time, using scientific approaches, put an end to the methods of self-deception in matters of sex and in this way, by improving our insight and making self-deception and trickery more difficult, reformed our sex attitudes and by the same token taught us how to cure morbid manifestations of the conflicts involved. He was even an important contributor to the practical disappearance of certain neurotic diseases like hysteria and war neuroses.

However, Freud's concentration on the role of libido in the normal and abnormal development of the individual forced him—and he was fully aware of this—to neglect somewhat the psychology of the Ego, which is of greater interest for the student of values. Freud's followers, including those who created their own 'schools' of psychotherapy, tried in various ways to complete Freud's ego-psychology. The third element of the human psyche besides libido and ego has the closest relation to our subject. It is Freud's super-ego, which is nothing but a system of values transmitted to us by society, largely and most early by our parents.[4] Here Freud has beeen severely criticized from various sides, since his case histories and his interpretations showed clearly that he accepted the contemporary middle class, Middle-European value systems as immutable and that they represented in most respects his own values. This contemporary criticism, first started by Russian communism, has been progressively growing as more and more of mankind's values have been undergoing changes. And yet Freud expected everything from science and science was supposed to be value-free.

I may mention here, as I have done elsewhere[5] that special doubts and self-doubts are frequent in psychotherapists who are trying to fulfill the postulate of value-free science. To give you two examples:

An investigation by Werner Wolf[6] showed that only 6% of psychotherapists considered a change of values in their patients as a goal. Grotjahn[7] on the other hand claims that the analyst does and should teach the patient certain values by identification with the analyst. Such are: patience, tolerance, devotion, empathy, intuition, tact, decency, modesty, loyalty, respect, carefulness, keeping distance, courage, honesty, frankness. And we do—I may add—occasionally see former analytic patients who have become copies of their analysts. The medical analyst also brings into the situation the value called 'medical ethics' which shows such curious little variations even from state to state.

This awareness of the analyst's own value system contains the best safeguard against introducing it too much into the objective view of the situation. It is something akin to the 'personal formula' of the astronomers.

It might be useful to point out that Freud was not simply a product of his contemporary values but also a product of the critique of then-existing value systems. In a recent article I pointed out the great influence which the philosopher Friedrich Nietzsche exerted in the 19th century on Freud, Adler and other contemporaries with his Re-valuation of All Values.[8]

If we shall discuss those areas of our mind relevant to the value problem and neglected by Freud it might be useful to concentrate on his first critic, Alfred Adler. In neglecting the others like Sullivan, Karen Horney, *etc.,* I shall not feel too guilty since they in their turn neglect to stress how many of their ideas were first expressed by Adler.

I shall disregard various differences, apparent and real, between the two men, Freud and Adler. Adler did not acknowledge the dominant role of sex and of the Oedipus complex; he did not acknowledge the subconscious and repression, only a 'non-understanding'; he was not interested in the cause but in the aim of the neurotic symptom or the dream; he assigned to the analyst a more active role in restoring the patient to normalcy. He agreed with Freud as to the important role which childhood plays in the development of our personality and in the necessity for the patient to understand his own false defenses, in the form of not understanding and sympton formation, which take the place of normal methods in dealing with the problems of life.

Adler sees man as born with deep-seated inferiority feelings, not to be confused with the symptom called 'inferiority complex,' a term coined by Adler. The only remedy against these inferiority feelings is striving either for power or for the preservation of a protective mother figure. In both cases a conflict arises not with Freud's super-ego but with the *'social feelings'* postulated by Adler. If these are strong enough a normal 'life style,' normal and efficient methods of dealing with the problems of life, develops. The task of the therapist is the awakening of those social feelings.

In analyzing my patients I tried to avoid as far as possible strict commitment to either Freud's or Adler's theory and to let myself be guided by the material presented by the patients' associations and dreams. Starting my practice in Freud's Vienna of the twenties and ending it in New York of the sixties I could not help but notice that in my earlier period Freudian mechanisms, in the later Adlerian mechanisms were prevalent. I explain this by the historical influence of Freud's teachings on our attitudes toward sex on the one hand and on the greater relevance of Adler's striving for power and his social feelings to the dominant economic, social, cultural problems of the present time. I came to the conclusion that in the unavoidable study of our changing values we cannot ignore Adler and those akin to him.

However, personally I am not ready to accept Adler's formulations as the best possible ones. I reject his universal 'inferiority feeling' which requires a process of judgment in favor of the universal 'basic anxiety' or 'existential anxiety' proposed by other authors.

> I, a stranger and afraid
> In a world I never made.
> *Housman.*

I fully accept the role of Adler's (or rather Nietzsche's[9]) 'will to power' in this situation which seems almost identical with Freud's ego strivings and fits in with the biologists' fight-flight responses, the instinct of self-preservation, the survival of the fittest, *etc.* The will to power is man's remedy for his basic anxiety. In human psychology it appears in innumerable forms, extending from the child's wish for omnipotence to the adult's immense variety of realistic, sometimes more concrete, sometimes more abstract, images of power.

The area of greatest and vital confusion is that of 'social feelings.' And yet here the need for clarification is the most urgent if we are to reach a deeper psychological understanding of values. Values, after all, are a social phenomenon. Adler himself was obviously groping for the right expression. He spoke of a *Geltungstrieb–Geltung* being a word of many meanings, from 'being acknowledged' to 'being very important'), later of *Gemeinschaftsgefuehle*–(feelings of community or for the community), still later of 'social feelings' and still later of 'social interest' (whatever this may be). Personally I could not corroborate his theory that development of social feelings leads to recovery. However, I frequently observed that with clinical progress the previously egocentric patient began to show social interest.

At any rate Adler's assumption of separate social feelings leads us straight into the old controversy between, say, Rousseau with his 'noble savage' and Freud who did not hesitate to ask 'Why should I love my neighbor?' It is in my opinion a most urgent task of psychoanalytically oriented psychology to resolve this problem once and for all, regardless of all ideological prejudices, cherished illusions, repressions and other abnormal defence mechanisms. This may take courage and determination, though perhaps less than we think. We are dealing here with the problem of acceptance of fear. Sports coaches, military instructors, *etc.* know very well what confusions and failures arise if trainees are told that they must not be afraid of the danger instead of not being afraid of fear.

Where to get the material for these studies? There are among clinical patients enough cases nowadays in which not sex but the relation to people is the central problem, and enough 'normal' people willing to be analyzed. In numerous cases—like in dealings with social groups other than our own—an open mind and curiosity centered on values *and their origins* is very helpful. In all these cases two pre-conditions are necessary: to have an open mind concerning the existence or non-existence of primarily social feelings and concerning values in general.

What else can serve as material for our studies? At present we can observe the development of social feelings in children and later in love and family relations; in a variety of cultures, in animals, in common emergency situations, in mass psychoses, in certain crises of social feelings like the present youth movements. But the most important subject of study will remain the individual. When does he lose his community feelings (social and sexual isolation is the most frequent factor in student suicides)? What happens in a conflict between two sets of community feelings (family vendetta in certain cultures)? What devices do we use to increase our social feelings (*e.g.* identification, 'imagine it happens to you') or diminish them (the cop-out, the criminal's conviction that it is all a swindle)? It seems self-evident that all these and many other vagaries of social feelings would have a decisive influence on our value systems.

It is important to realize that social feelings seem to be a very powerful defense against basic anxiety, perhaps second only to the will for power (the latter goes—in contrast to social feelings—beyond the fear of people alone). A boy, say, of eight comes to a new school or a new neighborhood. He will be afraid of the strangers who appear to him as a unified group. He watches their ball game, powerless. Suddenly they ask him whether he can catch. He says yes, he is a good catcher. From there on his fear of the group disappears because he knows he is *needed*. Being needed is a social feeling, one of the most important, and the psychiatrist is very familiar with the deep anxieties and depressions in melancholics, old people, *etc.* based on the feeling of not being needed. In the present youth unrest the lack of the feeling that one is needed certainly plays a role; we observe the attraction of such situations as the Peace Corps, the harvest in Cuba, *etc.* In the childhood memories of great leaders we often find the situation that the boy had to help his widowed mother, *etc.* The question is worth investigating whether in less advanced farming communities where the children's help is needed the social feelings are stronger and whether in the unwanted, and so not needed, child there is a special deficiency in social feelings. Some data seem to support this. A serious question arises: if being needed is one of the important devices against our basic fear of people and a basis of our social feelings how will they be affected by the emergence of a cybernetic society which might need people less and less? And how will this affect our value systems?

We know, for example, that values originate, change and will continue to change with changing social, economic, political, historical, educational conditions. They are in many instances the product of a tacit or open 'social contract.' On the other hand there are values which are tricks, self-deceits, ego-saving devices of individuals or groups of individuals. They are subconscious defense mechanisms similar to those used by neurotics. While in one culture high education, intellect, genius are worshipped (and that is even true in Communist Russia), in another (U.S.A.) the egghead is derided, the most insignificant worker may have a printed sign 'Silence, genius at work' and the 'mad scientist' is a favorite figure in cartoons and movies. This devaluation of intelligence is obviously a defense mechanism of the mediocre.

It is a fact that we possess certain depth-psychological data concerning the role of libido and ego, their conflicts with each other, the role of the infantile super-ego (the introjected value system of parents), the mature super-ego (the introjected demands of society) as far as they refer to values. True, this knowledge is quite incomplete as yet. There is a heated controversy about a subject very relevant to our problem: the existence or non-existence of true aggressive drives (or Freud's death instincts) in man and even in animals.

Would such knowledge help us to understand the origin of values? Do they actually derive not from our own instincts but exclusively from the demands of the society on these instincts? Does the preference for fat women in one century and country and for thin in the other, for much sex in one and little sex in the other period of history stem from changes in our libido? From changes in the demands of the society? Caused by what? Are the changes and rules imposed on our will for power based on enlightened self-interest? On a social contract? Or

c

are Adler and other successors of Freud right in assuming that there is some need in us, some drive to preserve and even develop society and certain relations to people? This is an old unresolved controversy concerning human nature which we mentioned before: the noble savage versus the absolute egotist.

Usually we assume that values are based on judgment but the suspicion is widespread that these judgments originate in or are strongly influenced by feelings.

As to the existence or non-existence of Adler's 'social feelings,' it is not even quite clear from Adler's writings whether we are dealing here with inborn or early acquired feelings. Adler strongly stresses the childhood influences on the development of those feelings. Are they universal? What is the external and internal evidence of these feelings? Are they primitive, sometimes never reaching consciousness? Or are they the product of more or less abstract thinking? Have we the right to say that a loner has no social feelings and a social butterfly has many? Is one of them sick?

We certainly would like to know more about the so-called herd instinct, so different in different animal species. We know practically nothing about the existence or non-existence of herd instincts in man— a problem certainly relevant to the psychology of values.

Let us illustrate the problem with two well known examples of people who occupy a prominent place in the cultural history of mankind.

Albert Einstein[10] wrote: '... there is one thing we *know*: that man is here for the sake of other men—above all those upon whose smile and well-being our own happiness depends, and also for the countless unknown souls with whose fate we are connected by a bond of *sympathy*. Many times a day I realize how much my own outer and inner life is built upon the labors of my fellow-men, both living and dead, and how earnestly I must exert myself in order to *give in return* as much as I have received. My *peace of mind* is often troubled by the *depressing* sense that I have borrowed too heavily from the work of other men.'

My inclination is to believe that these are not thoughts and feelings *resulting* from a certain value system but that rather the reverse is true: 'social' feelings and thoughts *leading* to a choice of values. However, I cannot prove it.

And yet the same Einstein writes: 'My *passionate* interest in social justice and social responsibility has always stood in curious contrast to a marked *lack of desire* for direct association with men and women.

I am a horse for single harness, not cut out for tandem or team work. I have *never belonged wholeheartedly* to country or state, to my circle of friends, or even to my own family. These ties have always been accompanied by a vague aloofness, and the *wish to withdraw* into myself increases with the years.' (italics mine).

Is this proof of lack of true social feelings, of a difference in values? Is only one of these attitudes true, the other a self-deceit? Again: we don't know enough to answer this question so relevant to the problem of values.

Another example is Thoreau, of whom Lewis Mumford[11] says: 'The more self-sufficient an individual seems to be, the more sure it is that, like Thoreau at Walden Pond, he carries a whole society in his bosom.'

Another variation of this, possibly abstract, kind of 'social interest' is H. G. Wells[12] who says: 'I do not believe in the least that either the body of H. G. Wells or his personality is immortal, but I do believe that the growing process of thought, knowledge and will of which we are part, and of which you are a part, may go on growing in range and power forever.'

And so all the way to the all embracing concepts of a Teilhard de Chardin[13] who holds that no elemental thread in the Universe is independent of all others.

If it were so it is peculiar that just great and famous men are more prone to see themselves as particles of a great community. Goethe said to Eckermann: 'If I could give an account of what I owe to great predecessors and contemporaries, there would be but a small remainder.' Thoughts or feelings?

The psychoanalyst will ask: are such abstract thoughts which must have a decisive influence on the formation of value systems based on some community feelings, instincts, drives? Or are they by any chance subconscious defense mechanisms against basic anxiety, as many suspect? The psychoanalyst does not yet have any definite answer. As far as *our consciousness* of such feelings is concerned there are certainly great individual differences. James Truslow Adams[14] thinks that only certain exceptional men have an *instinctive* appreciation of morality; the others need laws. No one will doubt that the degree of presence of that feeling, conscious or subconscious, of a *common cause* with all of humanity, past, present and future will have a powerful influence on the formation of values. They would also point to the necessary existence of some *permanent* values.

The individual's drive for power is not basically antisocial. Those who follow von Bertalanffy's General System Theory, as psychiatrists increasingly do, will easily understand that useful and necessary drives may become destructive of the system (including the individual himself) if they are out of proportion, if they disturb the harmony of the system. This is even true for social feelings (see the fanatic reformers, the do-gooders, the "bleeding hearts").

This is not to underestimate the tremendous potential anti-social effect of the drive for power; *e.g.* the most frequent and most cruel killings are family murders and their motivation is mostly the drive for power.

Wherever I stop the ending will be arbitrary. I have subjected you to the frustrating experience of realizing how great our area of ignorance is in the depth psychology of values. However, so little has been done in this respect, that we are entitled to optimism rather than to pessimism. Periods of transition in value systems are perhaps particularly suitable for such work as Freud's example shows in the area of sex. However, the psychoanalyst will expect here as in other areas strong resistances and defenses, some of which appear in the form of so-called 'vested interests,' some in other forms. In our era of progressive changes in value systems and the resulting turmoil this task of the psychoanalysis of values becomes all the more urgent.

Notes and References

1. Schilder, P. *Medical Psychology*, International University Press, New York, 1953.
2. Adler, A. *Social Interest, a Challenge to Mankind*, Capricorn Books, New York, 1964.
3. Dewey, J. In *Living Philosophies*, The World Publishing Company, Cleveland, New York, 1931.
4. Wilder, J. 'Beyond Parents: Parents as a Socioeconomic Phenomenon,' in S. Lesse, Ed., *An Evaluation of the Results of the Psychotherapies*, Ch. C. Thomas, Springfield, Ill., 1968.
5. Wilder, J. 'Values and Psychotherapy,' *Amer. J. Psychother*. 23, 405, 1969.
6. Wolff, W. 'Fact and Value in Psychotherapy,' *Amer. J. Psychother*. 8, 466, 1954.
7. Grotjahn, M. 'The Role of Identification in Psychiatric and Psychoanalytic training,' *Psychiatry*. 12, 141, 1949.
8. Wilder, J. 'Alfred Adler in Historical Perspective,' *Amer. J. Psychother*, 1970.
9. Nietzsche, F. *The Will to Power*, Vintage Books, New York, 1967.
10. Einstein, A. In *Living Philosophies*, The World Publishing Co., Cleveland, New York, 1931.
11. Mumford, L. In *Living Philosophies*, The World Publishing Comp., Cleveland, New York, 1931.

12. Wells, H. G. In *Living Philosophies*, The World Publishing Comp., Cleveland, New York, 1931.
13. Teilhard de Chardin, P. *The Future of Man*, Harper & Row, New York, 1964.
14. Adams, J. T. see under 12.

Some Psychological Presuppositions
of the Concept of Virtue:
A Case Study in the Relation
of Science and Ethics

ABRAHAM EDEL

The City College of City University of New York

The concept of *virtue*, together with that of *good* (value) and that of *obligation* (right, duty), are the Big Three in the history of ethics. When John Laird published his *An Enquiry into Moral Notions*, (1935), it seemed obvious to parcel the field into the theory of 'aretaics,' 'agathopoeics,' and 'deontology.' But this was the learned-historian perspective. In fact, *virtue* had long receded (at least among the philosophers) from its eminence in ancient ethics and in 18th century ethics, bowing out to *good* and to *obligation*.

The three concepts have no doubt systematic relations. Moral concepts have a collective job to do, and if one recedes, the others take over—or perhaps the one recedes because the others are driving it out. Now just as military strength cannot be understood without the economic and industrial base, so the meta-ethical relations of ethical concepts cannot be understood without seeing the background economy. This background is psychological and cultural as well as methodological and intellectual. Contemporary philosophers have paid attention chiefly to the latter group, and the analysis of ethical concepts has been guided chiefly by epistemological considerations. The present paper wants to straighten the bent stick by bending it back in the other direction. I choose the concept of *virtue* as a case study because its theoretical eclipse is itself an interesting phenomenon, because its psychological presuppositions are closer to the surface, and because there is some tendency today in philosophical circles to revive the concept. The same kind of job could be done for *good*—in fact, Dewey did it—by looking to the underlying psychological theory of purposive action and goal-seeking, which in effect calls the meta-ethical tune for this concept. *Obligation* (right duty) has been, on the whole, more resistant to such analysis because of the sheer complexity of the strands that are built into it.

A few historical notes will be helpful. The basic starting-points for the analysis of *virtue* are to be found on the one hand—the moral-code side—in the veritable parade of virtues on the face of human social history; on the other hand—the theoretical or, if you like, the meta-ethical side—in the diversity of philosophical treatments of the concept.

The descriptive parade need not occupy us long. For we are all generally familiar with the panorama of different virtues that have been central in different societies, cultures, sub-cultures. We may recall: the Greek cluster of wisdom, courage, temperance, justice; the Spartan war-virtues of courage, discipline and obedience, taciturnity, dogged adherence to tradition, loyalty, as contrasted with Athenian individualism, receptivity to the novel, attitudes of freedom and equalitarianism, readiness to discuss and to exercise initiative; the medieval Christian outlook with a stress on inwardness, purity, love, obedience, patience, humility, and the familiar history of vices that issue in the deadly sins; the Calvinist-puritan ethic with its constellation of thrift, diligence, sobriety, justice, sexual purity, and the striving for success in one's calling; the liberal virtues of individualism, initiative, creativity, independence, readiness to change, prudence, rational orderliness, humanitarian equality, and so on. These are bare suggestions of a wealth of constellations in the western world alone, to which the study of other areas of the globe and the comparative study of primitive cultures can add tremendous variety. If, however, some philosophers among us would rather consult the dictionary than the spread of history and comparative culture, they can find an equally extensive list, though less organized. For example, among the a's alone one can get going with: abject, abstemious, abusive, affable, ambitious, amiable, *etc.*

The diversities of theoretical analysis reflect the general philosophical approaches, as they seek a unified understanding of the concept. Yet they also show clearly, when lined up, how the presupposed psychology of the soul or the self furnishes the guidelines within which the concept is developed. Thus Plato starts off, in the Socratic dialogues, by asking whether all the virtues are really forms of knowledge; he ends up with a whole theory in which the unity is found in the soul's quest for the Good, and the several virtues then reflect the different parts of the soul in their effort to carry out their functions.[1] In general, teleological philosophies look to virtues as the ordered dispositions or states of character which will enable the human being to achieve the good. Aristotle[2] analyzing virtue into its genus and differentia in order to furnish a formal definition, locates the genus as *state of character*. The differentia he finds to be *aiming at the mean*. Accordingly, he analyzes each virtue by locating first the raw materials built into the character-trait, such as feelings of fear and confidence blended in some degree in courage, or social activities of giving and taking integrated in liberality. The differentia is seen in the formula that governs the blending: if the mean is achieved we have the virtue of courage, if excess in one or the other direction we have the vices of timidity and rashness; so too for liberality as against prodigality and miserliness. Aristotle's analysis ends up with a plurality of virtues, each constituting a stable relatively isolated system in its operation, fully actualized in the virtuous man and embodying a more difficult balance in the continent man. In the later development, in the utilitarian philosophies, there is a similar structure for virtue. Stable character traits are formed, under the operations of association as the psychological principle according to which experience settles into patterns; in the case of virtues as qualities of a person, the governing principle is that of utility, that is, character traits whose operation yields the general well-being.

There is another tradition in ethical theory which gives a less set and less dispersed account of virtue. The psychological base is some more unified, more central process that is going on and lies at the heart of being a man. Virtue becomes narrowed into one supreme effort. Thus in ancient Stoicism,[3] the spirit in its pursuit of serenity and independence wages a continual internal war not to attach itself to what is beyond its power; virtue lies solely in effective detachment. In Augustine too[4] there are no achieved virtues that can bask in their intrinsic worth and be desired on their own account, for such would be vices inflated with pride; the moral worth of every act lies in the character of the will embedded in it. Similarly, in Kant virtue is a moral strength of the will. The concept of virtue enters Kant's ethical scheme at a late point. A holy will has been defined as one governed completely by the moral law, and obligation has its origin in the act that men are moved by inclinations that are in conflict with the moral.[5] The task of continuous progress toward the unattainable ideal of the holy will is morally enjoined on men.[6] Hence, as Kant tells us in his *The Metaphysical Princi-*

ples of Virtue, virtue lies in a continuous battle in which it is always at the starting-point and in which not to advance is to lose ground.[7] Again, in Nietzsche, though in a quite different sense, it is will that is seeking expression now as domination; hence virtues express nothing more than the quality of dimineering strength or weakness.[8]

There is a third tendency in the philosophical presentation of virtue in which the focus is shifted from the cultivation of stable traits in the pursuit of the good or the quality of the inner struggle to the milieu of sociocultural interaction. Virtue is approached in terms of men's appreciative and critical responses to human behavior, but along different lines. Eighteenth century moralists, under the spell of the Newtonian model, looked for the underlying laws governing the responses and moved toward utilitarian theory.[9] Contemporary phenomenology takes the appreciative response to be the apprehending of values of personality, and looks for the essence in each cluster of virtues.[10] The materialist and naturalist approaches move toward a socio-cultural base for understanding virtues; virtues on this view are patterns of character or self stabilized and approved because of the institutions and forms of goal-striving they support. In Marxian historical materialism, they are tied to the class-formations and in evaluation to the direction of social development.[11] Dewey, accepting the shifting content of virtues and the fact of unavoidable constant change, redefines the concept in methodological terms to indicate the central features required in the expression and pursuit of human interest.[12]

In spite of this long tradition, it is striking that twentieth century philosophy does very little with the concept of virtue. Sometimes it is reduced to a sub-class of values: virtues are values of personality alongside of social values, action values, religious values, *etc.* More often, in analytic approaches, it is wholly subsumed under obligation. For example, E. F. Carritt says: 'If we define virtuous dispositions as those which lead people to do impulsively and effectively what reflection would generally or often show to be obligatory we seem nearer the truth.'[13]

This twentieth century eclipse of the concept of virtue can be seen to stem from both methodological and psychological considerations.

One very important cause was the positivist restriction on metaphysical entities in which such notions as self were swept away and even dispositional terms had for a time difficulty in surviving. The fear was that the language of potentiality or power or disposition would be used in explaining the phenomena, yielding obscurantist accounts. Bentham long ago had already described a disposition as fictitious entity, attempting to express what is permanent in a man's frame of mind.[14] Because the idea of character or self or personality is constitutive within it, the notion of virtue was particularly susceptible to this attack. The extreme psychological behaviorism of the earlier part of the century had the same effect. Once we translate the language of virtue into specific sets of acts, then the ethical apparatus which deals with right acts or obligatory acts hopes to handle the materials without any additional theoretical concepts.

The empirical critique of the concept of virtue has often leaned heavily on Hartshorne and May's *Studies in Deceit*.[15] These investigators carried out tests of honesty behavioristically. They gave maze puzzles in which the subject was cheating if he kept his eyes open; they asked students to mark their own test papers and had paraffin–paper techniques for detecting where the student corrected his previous answers; they asked subjects to check books read and included false titles on the list; and so on. Because there was insufficient correlation of results in diverse tests, they concluded that deceit is not a unified trait. Deceit and honesty are rather specific functions of life situations; deception is a method of adjustment used by a child when conflict arises in the environment. Qualities of man as an organized socially functioning self, not isolated virtues, distinguish a good man from a bad one. Transactional or situational qualities rather than intra-psychic traits fit the picture of the results.

To this shift in perspective was added the anthropological concept of cultural patterns, impinging on the relatively plastic child in the process of his growth.[16] Institutional and cultural forms and the practices and goals they embody furnish the unity of character. The outcome is, of course, men of a given sort, but both the explanatory principles for understanding that sort and the normative principles for evaluating it are socio-cultural. A major practical base of the concept of virtue has always been the fact that new generations arise and education is required to develop character. Education itself, however, may find that it does not do this job successfully by concentrating on the formation of single traits, associating praise or dispraise with them. It may find that it makes more progress if it cultivates insight, or uses role-playing to develop sensitivity in understanding others' position in human situations. Thus there may be no distinctive role left for the concept of virtue—except perhaps for intellectual virtues. The materials may be better cut and sorted along the lines of other concepts.

This stage in the history of the concept of virtue constituted a low ebb. It seemed that methodological, scientific, and practical considerations combined to render the concept useless and even misleading—to say that a child did not steal because he was honest was no better than the old jibe that opium put one to sleep because it possessed the dormitive principle. Still, this was not the end of the story. But the philosophically significant point is that the factors that came to the aid of the concept were of the same type as those that had shunted it aside. To these we must now turn.

First, there was a methodological retreat on the strictness of positivism and extreme behaviorism. Dispositional terms became reestablished with methodological finesse, and generally, it became permissible to construct theoretical terms and leave open as a separate issue whether the particular ones should be given a realistic interpretation (as 'atoms' and 'genes' eventually were) or a purely instrumental interpretation for purposes of calculation and systematic simplification (which is all one could claim for 'average man' or 'gross national product'). What was purged was obscurantism. As Laird had pointed out in the case of *virtue* as early as 1935: ' ... there is no good reason for regarding a man's moral character as a deep and holy well in which all that really matters is a secret sediment at the bottom. If the moral character were a name for the *unknown* cause of his moral thoughts and actions, it would indeed be secret and mysterious by definition; for it would be an unknown quality. But if it is essentially a statement of our knowledge about what *would* happen as well as an account of our knowledge about what *has happened* in the moral way there is nothing more mysterious about virtue and moral character than about anything else that concerns morality.'[17]

Such an account does not settle the question of the viability or utility of the virtue concept; rather it leaves the settlement open to scientific and theoretical investigation. In abstract terms it leaves us with the following situation. Each of the big three ethical concepts would appear to have some type of linkage to a sub-set of psychological phenomena. *Good* is linked to appetites, desires, purposes, pleasures, *etc.*, whatever the precise logical character of the linkage; the concept is viable if there is sufficient stability in this sub-set, whether a stability of goals or of criteria for ordering and evaluating goals. *Obligation* is linked to phenomena of 'conscience'—a range of feelings and phenomenological qualities—as well as to rules and practices functioning to regulate claims within the group; and similar issues of logical analysis and of stability arise as in the case of *good*. *Virtue* is linked to idea of character, personality, self-pattern. The question is whether these three sub-sets of psychological phenomena are relatively independent or whether they constitute a systematically related field. And if the latter is the case, the further question becomes pertinent, whether the concept of virtue is in some way reducible to the other concepts (or any of the three to the other two) so that its properties and the phenomena to which it is linked are explicable by the others and their associated phenomena. The viability of the concept of virtue is thus a special function of the kind of results we get in the scientific exploration of character, personality, self.

It is to be noted that the kind of stability and relative independence a viable concept of virtue would possess need not be that of a separately existing entity. It is quite compatible with virtue being a function of the total state of a field. Suppose it is granted, and indeed it seems very likely, that the concepts and phenomena we are dealing with constitute a systematic field. Or in general, let it be granted that any individual (thing or person, property or trait) is part of a wider milieu so that all ultimate explanation of its behavior or its special features is in principle a function of the total field. It may still be the case that, given certain constancies in the field, the behavior of one element in the field can then be understood in terms of its internal state alone. Even in the physical domain there will be differences of such a sort. The smoothness of a sheet of paper may be a function of the moisture of the field, if it is isolated, but of the weight on top of it, if it is at the bottom of a ream. On the other hand, the hardness of a metal may be usefully seen as a function of its inner constitution as long as the temperature fluctuates only within certain limits; near the surface of the sun its hardness would not be a comparably useful concept, but in practical technological contexts and in ordinary scientific contexts it may do. So too for *virtue,* if the field conditions are of the requisite sort. Let me take a few illustrations from the psychological literature which might seem to have a bearing on the answer. The aim here is not to give a conclusive answer but to restructure the way questions about virtue have been discussed in order to show how an answer may be sought. In this sense, the paper is (alas) simply programatic.

First, then, for the concept of character. On the whole, it has been criticized as too commonsensical, too crude, to bear the burden of scientific work and philosophical precision. Lawrence Kohlberg[18] has criticized the virtues and vices found in the conventional language as turning moral character into a 'bag of virtues'; he relies largely on the Hartshorne and May results and kindred studies to affirm its lack of utility. Dewey's treatment of character as a set of habits[19] has the same pluralism as the Aristotelian and the common conception, but Dewey's view of habit is more dynamic; when we recall that he gives intelligence a reconstructive role in the problem-situations where habits are in conflict, and that he uses the notion of habit in a stretchy way to cover the idea of self as well as that of intelligence itself, habit would seem to get us not far beyond the idea of relatively stable congeries of dispositions whose stability depends on the dynamics of the field. Gordon Allport, it is interesting to note, regards character as an evaluative concept; he says; 'Character is personality evaluated, and personality is character devaluated.[20] If this is so, then the notion of virtue can have no greater stability than that of personality.

How far will the scientific exploration of personality carry us in our search? Allport, after examining fifty definitions, settles on 'Personality is the dynamic organization within the individual of those psychophysical systems that determine his unique adjustment to his environment.'[21] This would not be very helpful to the concept of virtue, for several reasons. It ties the study of personality to the study of differences, rather than to the constancy of a pattern among individuals; traditionally, at least, a man does not grow his own special virtues, but is praised for having the ones that are hoped for among all men. (Would it be logically inconsistent to say that all men had the same personality, or would one then have to say that man lacked personality?) Again, the reference to psychophysical systems assumes the constancy can be exhibited in the physiological and psychological terms; the kinds of constancies appropriate to virtues might very well require cultural and socio-historical terms as well. In a more comprehensive formulation of personality by Kluckhohn and Murray,[22] prefatory to a collection of studies on all behavioral-science levels, the conception of personality is cast more in terms of certain functions to be carried out in a human being; it is the constancy of these functions which gives unity to the concept. Illustrations are: reduction of conflict by scheduling, by social conformity, by identification; reduction of aspiration tensions; and so on. Human personality is treated as a formation embodying a compromise. The analogue for virtues in moral theory might very well be to list a set of functions in internal organization and in interpersonal relations and in goal-pursuit, and see the virtues as appropriate modes of internal harmonization, of reducing interpersonal conflict, of regulating aspiration, and all of these stabilized as habits of individuals.

Along such lines, one would be tempted to look for some deeper constellation, in which personality takes its origin—for example, a depth account of the ego and ego-functions. In fact it seems as if the resurgence of the idea of personality itself drew considerable strength from the psychoanalytic theory of determinants. For the latter conveyed the promise that internal operations would be found distinctive enough to secure a patterned outcome whatever the external (socio-cultural) factors; this was, in effect, a promise that psychological constancies would be established across historical-cultural lines. And even where culturally variant character-traits were to be found, their significance would lie not in the differences so much as in the role they played in the internal economy. This was the way, for example, in which in the earliest Freudian formulation, attention had been focused almost exclusively on the inner career of libidinal energies. Again, the Freudian theory of succeeding oral, anal, and genital stages in child development tied specific virtue patterns to each; for example, orderliness, frugality, obstinacy, punctuality, cleanliness, were regarded as anal traits. We have here a multiple thesis. In part it is causal: particular zones become at different times the focus for discharge of excitation, and the situation of toilet-training becomes the mode of interpersonal relation in which the designated traits arise. In part it is diagnostic: excessive rigidity in these traits is taken to involve an original disturbance at that particular stage of development. Perhaps it is also phenomenological: no one wholly leaves behind earlier stages, so that normal exercise of these character traits involves some of the emotional quality of its origins. Contemporary work has developed such an approach with greater attention to the permeation of cultural factors. Erikson, in his *Childhood and Society*,[23] continues the developmental orientation; he finds critical steps in the child's progress, mastering of which is productive of basic character-attitudes. Thus when the infant successfully lets his mother out of sight without undue anxiety or rage, we have the achievement of trust as against basic mistrust; experiences in connection with major bodily functions show us the setting in which autonomy is developed as against shame and doubt, and initiative is developed as against guilt; and so on. Cumulatively there is the development of individual identity and ego integrity. The psychological traits here involved are readily recognizable as the content of major virtues in moral usage. Erich Fromm, in his *Man for Himself*,[24] attempts directly to construct character-types through fusion of psychoanalytic and cultural categories—for example, the exploitative orientation in which a man takes by force and cunning, or the marketing orientation in which a man experiences himself as a commodity with self-esteem depending on the extent to which he can sell himself. Abram Kardiner's concept of a basic personality[25] also attempts a fusion: he points to a relatively stable constellation of traits in each people expressing largely the individual's early familial relationships and methods of rearing. These play a secondary role alongside of primary economic relationships, and are reflected most clearly on a large-scale screen in the projective non-reality systems of folklore, religion, etc. The basic personality constitutes, in effect, the psychological profile of the society.

Such approaches appeared to be stepping-stones in the attempt to develop a more integrated model for the study of personality which would take account of the social and cultural and historical as well as the biological and inner-psychological. The shape of the outcome is not yet clear; no doubt it depends on the general form that an integrated theory of behavioral science will take. In more recent psychological study the concept of the self has reemerged as an inclusive concept, of which the ego is one part, and focus lies on the growth and patterning of the self-system in response to nature and society. Comparative anthropological study (as in the work of Hallowell[26]) shows the norms which get built into the self: modes of self-reference, location of position, sense of the self in time, inter-personal orientation, *etc.* Psychological study turns to direct features of the self-system. For example, the current work of Witkin and others[27] relates perception and cognition to personality; it distinguishes the field-dependent and field-independent characteristics of individual selves and examines the conditions of self-formation which achieve weak or strong boundaries between the self and the field. Current studies of shame and guilt in this context interpret them clearly as modes of response in self-formation and self-regulation, rather than as emotions with a life of their own.[28] And studies of sensory deprivation and effects of drugs probe for chemical bases and differential psychological effect on the self. Such comprehensive studies, as well as the socio-cultural work on the relation of self-forms to institutions and social practices, considerably enrich the concept of self and increasingly give substance to the concept of virtue as prefigured in the more dynamic moral philosophies we noted above.

It is in terms of the outcome of such developments that the viability of the concept of virtue in moral philosophy has to be settled. There is no point in forcing it. Any purely philosophical formulation would constitute in effect a projection of possible results, and would be tested by subsequent actual results. If the basic psychological picture that emerges has room for relatively independent self-features over and above a focus on the transactional character of self-expression—given specific constancies in the field relations—then the virtue concept is worth restoring to central importance.

Let me speculate a bit on possibilities. Under what field conditions would the concept of virtue become critically central to moral philosophy? Under what conditions would it become wholly inapplicable? Under what conditions would it have limited specific application? Here we have to recall the initial emphasis on its systematic relations with other ethical concepts. Suppose the non-self portion of the moral field becomes so complex and so changing that there could be no stable rules of obligation and no stable goals to serve as guides in regulating conduct. Short of an intuitive theory to deal with immediate situations each on its own, moral philosophy might seek to find its stability in the maintenance of a certain kind of self. This is, in effect, the Stoic model; or the situation in which the only moral advice we can give is to consider all the facts, be sincere in one's judgment, and so on. It is worth noting here that Kohlberg's criticism mentioned above is operative only against very specific virtues—in fact, his own theory of moral development leans heavily on ego factors of growing insight and intellectual development, which in the old Aristotelian language would have been described as 'intellectual virtues'! Suppose, now, on the other hand, that there are stable goals, even if only in the minimal sense of the ones necessary for survival, but the complexities and flux of human existence bear heavily on the self. This is an extreme supposition, apparent only in extreme cases. For example, Robert Lifton's recent picture of 'protean man'[29] is generalized from the kind of total shifts of self-form that he found to characterize subjects in Asia who had undergone successive upheavals. Especially in Chinese subjects he found shifts under extreme stress from older ways to revolutionary selves, to counter-revolutionary selves, in each period with a total transformation. Lifton thinks this kind of protean man is the emerging self-pattern, given the conditions of the contemporary world. Now under these conditions, short of some notion of the intrinsic value of the passing self-forms, moral philosophy would have to center moral guidance on a basic goal-orientation, rather than a virtue-orientation or an obligation-orientation.

Finally, what are the practical needs, resting on constancies in the field of human life under the shape it seems likely to take in the contemporary world, which might support a limited set of virtues of different sorts on different levels of generality? I suspect very much that the level of generality that will crumble is the middle range one—the virtues that have a degree of conduct referred to which is too specific for the changing situation and insufficiently broad for generalized guidance; examples would be the virtues of patriotism in its national reference, chastity in its Victorian sense, obedience in its unreflective accepting sense. But both highly general and highly specific virtues may still have a central place. Respect for others, loyalty as a sense of commitment, sincerity in interpersonal relations, a sense of responsibility for others, collective participation in common welfare, and so on, would exemplify the broad type. Many of these would almost have the kind of generality which would give them a constitutive place in self-formation, alongside of the characteristics of ego-strength like a sense of realism and an ability to see a situation from other than the immediate perspective. On the other hand, the very specific virtues would be tied to very specific necessities of the existent mode of life; for example, care and caution in complex technology might have the absolute character that punctuality often sought in an industrial plant; precision and clarity may have a comparable base. In these senses, virtues may continue to have a place in the common-sense way in which they have played a part in education. But instead of constituting a miscellaneous bag they will each come with an explanatory and justifying preamble, pointing to the constancies and necessities on which they rest.

It is worth noting that in these respects the problem of virtues is quite parallel to that of generalizations in obligation and in the good. There have been attacks on the notion of rules in moral obligations in specific situations as misleading by holding up the hope of a systematic classification of duties and deductive applications to particular cases. Thus Dewey condemned rules (in the sense he used the concept) in favor of principles of analysis. Recently there have been attempts to reinstate rules in a constitutive sense, on the assumption that morality is carrying on an enterprise and every enterprise, like every game, has its constitutive rules which tell you how to carry it on or play it, as distinct from its rules that simply epitomize its lessons of experience about how to play it well. Generalization concerning obligations may very likely have the same outcome I have suggested for virtues—viability for the highly general (almost constitutive) and for the very specific, where strict adherence is required by the state of life. On the other hand, in the case of the good, it is the most general goals that have proved empty, (*e.g.,* the idea of happiness, or of pleasure) and the middle-range and the very specific seem to be coming into their own.

I suggest as a concluding diagnosis of the concept of virtue, in the light of its psychological and socio-cultural bases as we have considered them, that it remains a good bet for fresh philosophical analysis and systematic revival. But this assumes there will be some degree of field stability, as well as some methodological sanity which does not insist on reducing everything to momentary states or all of value theory to instantaneous preferences in momentary choices; and it points attention to pragmatic factors or practical needs of the age as part of the determining factors. In short, the concept of virtue has to be dealt with not in terms of linguistic uses alone or of common-sense psychology, but in terms of the results of the fuller scientific picture of the underlying phenomena to which the moral concepts are linked.

There is a final warning which must always be kept in mind. As knowledge of the underlying phenomena advances it is always possible that the materials underlying virtues and the materials underlying obligations (either with values or all together) may yield a unified picture at a deeper level, and be parcelled out in a novel way; if so, new concepts may make inroads on both virtue and obligation. Something like this seems to be happening when the idea of *commitments* as both expressing self-formations and issuing in obligations straddles the field of the older divisions. Even without something like this happening, and with maintenance of the present Big Three and their linkage to the psychological phenomena explored, it is possible that some hitherto neglected component may rise to the top and take its place alongside— conceivably emotion and feelings alongside of the entrenched phenomena, though it does not seem likely in the light of present psychological theories of emotion. Or again, a deeper discovery of functional relations among the components may gear one of the concepts to the service of another—as, for example, virtues have so often been geared to basic social aims in the historical parade we surveyed above. Whatever the long-range outcome in the politics of ethical categories, we will never be able to make sense of conceptual changes unless we see them as subject to the same kind of analysis as we have here been pursuing for virtue.

Notes and References

1. Plato. *Republic*, esp, Bk. IV.
2. Aristotle. *Nicomachean Ethics*, esp. Bks. 2–4.
3. *E.g.* Epicteus. *The Manual* (included in *Essential Works of Stoicism*, by Hodas (ed.), New York: Bantam Books, 1961).
4. *E.g.* Augustine. *The City of God*, Boston: Houghton Mifflin, 1943, Bk. XIX, 25.
5. Kant, Immanuel. *Foundations of the Metaphysics of Morals*, New York: Liberal Arts Press, trans. L. W. Beck, 1959, pp. 30–31.
6. Kant, Immanual. *Critique of Practical Reason*, Liberal Arts Press, trans. L. W. Beck, Indianapolis: Bobbs-Merrill, 1956, p. 33.

7. Library of Liberal Arts. Trans. Ellington, Indianapolis: Bobbs-Merrill, 1964, p. 69.

8. Nietzsche, Friedrich. *The Genealogy of Morals.* Garden City, N.Y.: Double-day Anchor Edition, 1956.

9. *E.g.* Hume, David. *An Inquiry Concerning the Principles of Morals,* New York, Liberal Arts Press, 1957.

10. *E.g.* Hartman. Nicolai. *Ethics,* New York: Macmillan, 1932, Vol. II.

11. *E.g.* Engels, Frederick. *Anti-Duehring,* New York: International Publishers, Ch. 9–10.

12. Dewey, John. *Theory of the Moral Life,* New York: Modern Library, 1930, Ch. 4.

13. *Ethical and Political Thinking,* Oxford: Clarendon Press, 1947, p. 85.

14. Bentham, Jeremy. *An Introduction to the Principles of Morals and Legislation,* (in *The Utilitareans,* Dolphin Books, Garden City, N.Y.: Doubleday and Co., 1961), Ch. 11.

15. Hartshorne, H., and May, M. A. New York: Macmillan, 1928.

16. *E.g. Ibid,* and Mead, Margaret. *Growing Up in New Guinea,* New York: William Morrow and Co., 1930.

17. Laird, John. *An Inquiry into Moral Notions,* London: George Allen and Unwin, 1935, p. 17.

18. 'Moral Development,' in *International Encyclopedia of the Social Sciences,* Vol. **10,** New York: The Macmillan Co. and The Free Press, 1968, pp. 483–494.

19. *Human Nature and Conduct,* New York: Modern Library, 1930.

20. Allport, Gordon W. *Personality,* New York: Holt, 1937, p. 52.

21. *Ibid,* p. 48.

22. Kluckhohn, Clyde, and Murray, Henry A. (eds.). *Personality In Nature, Society and Culture,* New York: Alfred A. Knopf, 1948, Chs. 1–2.

23. Erickson, Erik H. *Childhood and Society,* New York: W. W. Norton, 1950, esp. Ch. 7.

24. Fromm, Erick. *Man for Himself,* New York: Rinehart and Co., 1947, esp. Ch. 3.

25. Kardiner, Abram, and associates. *The Psychological Frontiers of Society,* New York: Columbia University Press, 1945. *Cf.,* also Hartmann's *Ethics, op. cit.*

26. Hallowell, A. I. *Culture and Experience,* Philadelphia: Univ. of Pennsylvania Press, 1955, esp. Ch. 4.

27. Witkin, H. A. and others. *Psychological Differentiation,* New York: John Wiley, and Sons, 1962.

28. *Cf.,* Lewis, Helen B. *Shame and Guilt in Neurosis,* New York: International University Press, 1970.

29. Lifton, Robert J. 'Protean Man,' *Partisan Review,* Winter, 1968, pp. 13–27.

Freedom and the Meaning of Mind

HERMANN WEIN

University of Göttingen

A short introduction

The subject matter of 'human freedom' has manifold connections with all kinds of different topics. Therefore I will try to reach the central problem by approaching it from different starting points. Part of the complex of the main subject includes the problems of 'mind' and 'value-orientation.'

First of all, let me put some heuristic questions. 'Where' is freedom? In the human mind? In the 'intelligible character' (Kant) of man?

Yet, are not these questions all simply part of an irrational mystification, and does not the same apply to similar questions about the concept of 'value'?

The English language provides two possible translations for the 'famous' (notorious) German word 'Geist.' It is Hegel who has made a philosophical concept out of this term, whereas up to Hegel's time it had preponderantly enjoyed a theological sense (*spiritus*). It is used by older psychologists roughly in the sense of 'mind.' Kant even uses *'Gemüt'* for its equivalent, which has an altogether different meaning in contemporary German. In the English language there is always a danger of confusing 'mind' with 'spirit'—that key-word of German idealistic metaphysics, which has always been conformable to theology. This very confusion has made history in the philosophy of modern times.[1]

As we can see in Kant's and Hegel's philosophies, freedom can almost become a synonym for the high-flown concept of the 'Absolute' in German idealistic speculation. Then 'free spirit,' as expressed in 'practical reason,' is locus for the supreme human values.

Marx, Nietzsche, Ludwig Wittgenstein, and Gilbert Ryle, have put an end to the German speculation upon the 'true meaning' of spirit. Once I overhead an English colleague exclaim: '... this horrible mixture of German beer and German metaphysics ...' But when Kant defined man's inner self, practical reason, as a recognition of 'free will,' he meant to maintain the autonomy of man against God. That means he attacked the notion that the supreme value-commands—the absolute Good—should be given to man by super-human and super-historical instance.

The communistic world defines freedom as 'recognition of necessity.' This was Spinoza's idea and Hegel and Marx transformed 'necessity' into 'historical necessity.' In this concept now, where is to be found the freedom of man. Man whose *actions* (more than anything else) constitute human *history*? I have, therefore, called the orthodox Marxist solution a declaration of the infallibility of history. The political impetus of this idea is a mortal threat to the so-called 'Free World' of the West.

In this confusion of terms I shall proceed along the way outlined in my own writings under the title of 'Philosophical Anthropology';—indeed, a 'big word' of a most awe-inspiring kind, as the Analytical School will justly claim. Yet for me on the contrary 'philosophical anthropology' is a reference—in connection with 'mind' and 'freedom'—to the secure foundations of freedom; a freedom that may be limited in many ways but nevertheless cannot be argued away, and without which man would not be Man. This last sentence does not express just another philosophical idea, but its meaning will presently be demonstrated pretty concretely, I hope. Philosophical anthropology means: being anti-idealistic without being materialistic;[2] neither metaphysics-from-above, which either posits values as 'ideal entities,' or analyses words with merely negative results, nor anti-metaphysics-from-below founded on matter and atomic movements. For in the latest physics matter 'gave up its spirit'—to employ a German saying in a deeper and more radical sense.[3]

In other words, not to believe in non-subjective circumstances that condition to a certain extent man's action and social life-process is just as old-fashioned as to believe *only* in scientific facts, expressed in observation sentences with factual meaning. They are both of them forms of fetishism: the one, a kind of idealistic spiritualism, the other, 'physicalism' of the Rudolf Carnap of the Twenties, which since then he himself has buried.

Non-restricted freedom vs. non-speculative value-theory

Freedom is not a fact; freedom is a postulate; as such it is necessary for man in order to sketch and delineate humaneness!

This in turn means, that it is a postulate for all who conceive of value-awareness in its *anthropological* sense; without there being any need for an explicit philosophical understanding. It can be explained as the concrete practical possibility man has to develop himself from just a part of nature that is completely governed by a non-human necessity into a being whose behavior is partly guided by conscious value-awareness. Sufficient empirical evidence for what we just said is yielded by Cultural Anthropology, which is a new science that is almost exclusively done in the United States. This science has recorded a great number of astonishingly different guiding systems for human behavior, which are therefore neither guided by instinct nor biologically programmed (cultural patterns).

I maintain: the subject-matter of human freedom has no longer anything to do with an apologetic metaphysics, whose task would be to defend such a thing as freedom against physical necessity or against the 'mechanism of Nature.' Kant's doctrine of freedom was put squarely up against the latter in order to constitute the *human* value of the human being.

Teleological, historical necessity is a vision of anti-metaphysicians, the most dreadful vision of the human mind that has ever made practical-political history and it continues to do so. For example, the missionary spirit of Soviet Imperialism certainly no longer operates in the name of Hegel's irresistible 'world spirit' (*Weltgeist*), but in the name of Moscow's 'objective laws of historical progress,' of orthodox historical materialism. These so-called laws *must* lead to the ultimate value-telos: 'the realm of freedom' (Marx). But Marx's cautiously vague formula has been dilectically distorted into the un-dialectical concept of a 'classless society,' by which the formidable lack of freedom in the communistic countries becomes a necessary station of the development of irresistable freedom in society—through a fetishistic interpretation aided by a concept of freedom warranting the result right from the outset.

I have heard of a German merchant who was living in the Manchurian town of Charbin when the Soviet Russian troops arrived there during their Two Day's War against Japan. He and the Russians were getting on well with each other, until one day he put this question to the Russians: 'What about freedom in the Soviet Empire?' The Russians' answer was: 'Only in our state is there genuine freedom. For, freedom means that people get what they desire. And we make sure that they desire what they are getting. . . .'

In today's philosophical anthropology we have to bring into focus man as the creator of human history without either exaggerating or deprecating what we call 'freedom' in this historical process. The genuine centre lies neither in those values that are based solely in the sphere of ideas nor, reversely, in those that are founded only in the sphere of the material world. Would there be a subject-matter for a philosophical anthropology at all without that 'X-factor' that we call freedom? Putting aside all kinds of dogmatic global theorems, I understand human history—a series of human self-alienations, in which process man, by realizing negative values, deprives himself of his own freedom.[4] Yet one likewise has to accept the series of revolutionary acts as ways of partly taking back self-alienation by broadening the human mind with regard to values.

This is identical with a highly limited 'freedom-*in*-history.' This concept associates the 'X-factor: mind' with the 'X-factor: freedom,' and does so not in the idealistic way of identifying both by using the concept of 'intelligible character' as does 'practical reason.' Of the concrete existence of these two we have no historical proof whatsoever, as far as our historical knowledge goes.[5] To be sure, fate, God, and the atoms and their causality are not limitations for such a freedom as is under discussion here. The 'freedom' of man to dehumanize himself threatens 'human freedom.' People are sometimes found to be 'pathologically necessitated' (Kant), especially if they have submitted themselves to the theorems of a super-human or extra-human necessity of history and have therefore not been able to genuinely get to themselves.

An instance of this might be found in Karl Marx's writings if they were studied in a sufficiently unorthodox way. Besides, there are people that have surrendered themselves to the forces of the Unconscious, the 'Id,' because their conscious minds are not strong enough to defy them (Sigmund Freud).

History affords us thousands of examples of the devastation of human freedom and, therefore does not refute it. Freedom should not be conceived as a mere theorem, but rather as a historically concrete postulate, relative to the empirical historical state of things; it is something whose play is confined within narrow limits. Whoever '*reasons*' about 'mind,' 'freedom,' and 'values' speculates beyond these limits and indulges in meaningless words. (That is what Kant means by '*vernünfteln.*') As a matter of fact, we always have to deal with specific historical-empirical instances of freedom such as those oriented towards 'human rights' and human dignity (values). Whoever tries to argue away these 'plays-within-limits,' because they are not conformable to his general theory, need not trouble himself with the categories 'mind' and 'values' at all. Whoever denies the existence of a certain form of freedom that phenomenally differs from the phenomenology of animal behavior, calling the former a straight away fictional, ideological speculation without in any way being concerned about its concrete reality, or whoever subsumes it under the superstructure either of a metaphysical-idealistic or a naturalistic-materialistic world-view, argues without regard to scientific method and its results. From the historically proved capability of man to dehumanize himself, freedom follows as a postulate. Summing up we can say: We measure man's value in terms of his self-development, his self-realization; and negative value as Man's losing himself. This I call the 'anthropological value-concept.'[6]

The anthropological value-concept

Freedom as the condition for the possibility of value-oriented behavior —or values as sub-hypotheses of the hypothesis of freely self-regulating behavior? That is the question man's life is lived within this circle.

To make this clear, some further considerations follow.

a) It is concrete historical freedom, not happiness, power, or pleasure that is the supreme *bonum humanum,* the supreme value. Here the question 'Good to what end?' does not make sense. We are dealing with something that is good in its own right, as the ultimate humanity of human life, and not only as a means for something else. Always granted, of course, that the empirically well-founded distinction between human and animal behavior is not thought of as a sort of specious rubbish. The subject we are discussing here is the specific quality that makes history 'history', a term that is blurred if not referred to man's way of acting.

My main thesis reads: one should try to make the idea clear—logically as well as gnoseologically—that the entire concept of a specific human behavior is rendered useless and turned into an 'idol' (Francis Bacon) by the elimination of any one of its constituents (i.e. 'mind,' 'freedom,' 'values'). Just in the same way the dogma of a universe totally governed by metaphysics or by laws of nature renders these same concepts superfluous.

b) The conceptual content of freedom—not of dogmatic speculation, but of 'philosophical anthropology' as constituted by a totalization of phenomena—must overlap with a further basic concept, *i.e.* 'self-determination.' This means a determination neither exclusively by natural determinants nor by supernatural guidance; or, to put it more positively, if there is a being that consciously makes decisions according to perspectives that are not previously determined by God or by nature ('values'), then there is only decision proper. It is this being that may be called an 'actor' in the precise sense that an actor develops his value-orientation towards a maximum of self-direction. What else should value-ethics be really about? It will not exclusively want to theorize about such unknown entities as 'values' or 'free will.' Nor will it consist of language analysis. Of course, we are no longer positing the absolute freedom of a divine value-fixing or of a Kantian intelligible autonomy, which once were the foundation of the supreme value.

In contradistinction to the more archaic formulae—'ethical principles' and 'maxims,' 'virtues' and 'commandments'—the active partaking in the creation of one's own historical and social life-sphere signifies something genuinely concrete. This, indeed, is why I call the instances of freedom 'interludes' in the course of instances of non-freedom. Freedom does not *exist* (*Freiheit ist nicht*). But if it was not a postulate there would be no *human* future. At least no future that is to a certain extent created by a human actor. Otherwise it could not have become the subject-matter of a fast-developing science, 'futurology' (science of future).[7]

This partially realizable self-determination is, really, the fundamentally characteristic difference between man and all kinds of entities that are determined either by instinct or by natural laws. Immortal soul, *logos,* spirit, a future society without man ruling over man? . . . ? Grand utopian visions, maybe, yet without concrete prospects!

Above I said that no further questions would make sense about the ultimate end of the realization of our limited freedom.

To be sure, one could answer to such a question: according to the theory of psychoanalysis it is the reinforcement of *Ego* against *Super-Ego* and *Id.* I should like to integrate this thought into the course of my reflections in the following way. The empirically verified role-playing entity that we call man comes into existence only through the conscious *Ego*'s susceptibility to values that are chosen as directives for its actions. This very interwovenness is the real state of things. The elimination of any one of the main categories would leave us with distorted ideas that either would glorify value or deny its function—both of which are irrational mystifications.

It is not so much psychology but rather the realm of historical facts that is the great experimental field for the subject of 'values and freedom.' That explains the following: we cannot talk about value-orientation (as a reality!) without talking about freedom at the same time. For we are not talking about some kind of value-judgment or about *meta*-ethics, in which merely the linguistic and analytical aspects are under discussion, but rather about 'value,' 'mind' and the specifically free, existential, and social dynamics of man, whose life we ourselves live. Therefore we have to put up with 'big words,' although the Oxford-school maintains that we should simplify them by language-analysis before using them. (Of this school's contribution to solving the problems of actual concrete freedom, I must confess, I am ignorant.)

Committed value-theory

Therefore we should inquire into the sober sense of what is called *'philosophie engagée'* in Europe. Only if we altogether neglected the complex of practical interrelations called man, could we believe in 'pure' science or 'analysis.' One wonders whether such an orientation ought to be called 'philosophy'? Philosophy from its very beginnings in history has, indeed, always been connected with improvements in value-awareness by way of improving mental capacities. Over against this conception of philosophy lurks the narrow conception of a purely theoretical 'Ism.' If we are not schizophrenic, we surely should not be expected to argue away scientifically, the very conception of the human being that we ourselves are constantly striving for.

We cannot offer a 'pure science' that would inform us of exactly what 'values,' 'freedom,' and the specifically 'human' are. Truth is to be found only in totality. To make that thought more concrete we will give implicative definitions of at least three expressions:

1) 'human freedom.' The adjective 'human' is not related to the noun 'freedom' in a formally logical way.

2) The complex concept is concretely realized in the sphere of 'ethics,' *i.e.,* in behavior that is not preponderantly guided by instinct. This has been proven by behaviorists as an empirical proposition by

means of a comparison between the structures of human and animal behavior.

3) The last-mentioned thought presupposes the employment of values as directives in the social life of the specific human kind:

I maintain that these concepts 'human' and 'freedom' inseparably belong together, although they ought not to be identified.

If one identifies them (freedom, ethics, the good), it produces an abstract idealism (*cf.* Kant's theory of the 'supreme good,' which is radically and rigorously separated from everything natural and concrete).

The starting point of our philosophical-anthropological-structural synthesis is—as has been pointed out—I) anti-idealism; although I do not, for instance, regard Kant and Hegel simply as idealists, except when dogmatically (mis-interpreted and simplified II), anti-materialism; for the 'materialists' strained misinterpretation of 'freedom' as the 'recognition of necessity' is fundamentally not human. The term 'value' gets eliminated as a bourgeois or an idealistic expression, or else as 'pure air,' *flatus vocis,* in the same way it did in the tradition of 'skeptical nominalism' from William of Occam to Ogden and Richards.

Over against these traditions I advance a 'synthesis'

Let me try to illuminate this synthesis by using the following paradox: 'the idealistic protest against idealism.'[8] I should like to interpret this curious formula in the following way: Marx was the idealist of our age *par excellence,* in spite of his own intentions, because, after all, he did not care so much about matter but rather about man (yet without the Kantian *absolutism* of freedom). The idealists, in the widest sense of this term are materialists in so far as they deal with values as if they were some special sort of entity instead of inquiring into their relations to specifically human, social behavior, which is the only way of concretely determining them. The synthesis I am putting forth consists in the inseparability of 'value' from natural, *i.e.* historical and social, man.

The mortal threat that we are encountering from both extremist ideologies I take as a proof of the necessity for a philosophical understanding and a synthesis of the complex totality.[9]

A provisional summing-up must read as follows: 'freedom' is part of a group of at least three concepts. For these only an 'implicative definition'—as mathematicians term it—is tenable; *i.e.,* each concept can only be defined by its relations to the two others, and this holds reciprocally; or, rather, it can be defined by the 'interdependence' (Whitehead) constituted by the whole structure, the grouping of the concepts, of which each one by itself is not a sufficiently clear indication.[10]

Concluding formulae

1)   The specific life-process of man—whose life we live *in praxi* ourselves—separates him from beings that are necessitated by natural forces only in a way that has been thoroughly investigated.

2)   The 'concrete reality' of a limited human freedom no longer represents a lofty 'big word.'

3)   This 'X-factor' in the interpersonal social life of the singularly human kind, *i.e.,* one that is not totally determined by somatic laws or bio-genetically programmed, makes the a-historical historical.

If we dropped any one of these three concepts we should need neither values nor human behavior-regulations. Then all this would be rubbish, of which the analytical school of contemporary philosophy would free us. But we do not depend on philosophies; only philosophers pretend that we do. What, then, does guide human behavior, if it isn't some kind of dogma? It is done by the interpersonal, social interplay of 'roles' that transform the merely biological into the human. Within this interplay, can be distinguished differing role-projects and various reciprocal role-expectations. And this interplay implies the 'X-factor' 'freedom' that has something to do with that other 'X' that we call 'mind.' Ethical situations are embedded and localized in this synthetical reality. We do not need a theory of values: in our acts we actualize a synthetic guiding system, in which the terms 'values,' 'freedom,' historical 'self-realization' are relative structural elements. There is no sober evidence for a structure of this kind in any entity of the universe other than man.

Thus expressions such as 'freedom' and 'values' cannot be separated from the typical human organization of action, for which 'value-orientation,' 'mind,' as well as 'reason' are abbreviations of long standing. Human intersubjectivity is empirically distinguishable from instinct-directed extra-human social life and exactly this *is* 'mind.'[11]

Thus we reach two propositions, which originally derive from german philosophy:

a) 'Freedom from . . .' is to be discerned from 'freedom for . . .'

b) Freedom means a 'plus of "determination".'

Three further propositions hardly need much argumentation:

A) I am compelled by my needs and so I am not free, regardless of whether these needs are conscious or unconscious.

B) I am free, if I act within the limitations set up by these needs according to roles that presuppose self-determination as the supreme value.

C) I have, yet, to consider the possibility, that the value-ethics under discussion has credit only in the historical context of our culture which stresses individualism. It is Nietzsche who first formed the plural of '*Moral*' in philosophical German, and who first inquired into the 'morality of *mores*' (*Sittlichkeit der Sitte*).

Although today we are talking of a plurality of systems that systematically guide our behavior ('*Werttafeln*', Nietzsche), there remains a historical possibility that we could fall back into the original state of a 'morality of *mores*,' into a kind of '*posthistoricum.*'[12] Or do we proceed to an 'oecomenical world culture,' which would transcend the 'provincial' moral systems by a widening of consciousness?

It remains to set forth the following scheme as a last interpretation of that 'plus of determination' which human freedom concretely realizes in behavior. Complete arbitrariness vs. constraint: both are meaningless extremes, if projected into the historical dimension.

Rationalized in history, they mean the tension between liberty and justice for. . . .

In the process of human development a value-orientation is required that is aware of the free play allowed to men by the dimension of their roles and that is open to their symbols.

'Free from . . .' is an expression that can be proved to be self-contradictory. For example, in his 'acts' Robinson Crusoe was in a condition completely lacking freedom; 'the terrible freedom of the blind,' or of a man who, having been exposed in a desert, is allowed to go wherever he wants (A. Camus, A. Saint-Exupery) surpasses concrete freedom.

A child is taught the rules of a game by us, and it has to obey them. Now, it is an empirical fact, that, if this child chose—for the sake of 'freedom'—not to take part in the interplay with the other children, it would be a most miserable, value-deprived child.

The traffic-sign is a concrete means of setting limitations upon our otherwise unruled car-driving. And yet, within these limitations there arises the freedom of driving wherever one likes—given that one does prefer one direction to some other.

Notes and References

1. English translations of Hegel's main work translate either 'Phenomenology of the Mind' or ' . . . of Spirit'.
2. Did Kant's critical 'restriction' mean anything else?
3. *Cf.* the 'matter–anti-matter' dispute of the latest nuclear research.
4. *Cf.* Hegel's dialectic of master and servant; or Sartre's 'We *live* our self-alienation', in 'Critique de la Raison Dialectique', Vol. I, Paris, 1957.
5. Kant shares the optimism of the Enlightenment in the tradition of Descartes-Locke-Hume-Leibniz. Like them, Kant, was an unhistorical thinker.
6. On 'empirical value-studies' *cf.* H. Wein, *Kentaurische Philosophie*, München 1968, 'Zur Integration der neuen Wissenschaften vom Menschen'.
7. During the last few months three institutes for futurology were founded in Munich.
8. Jean-Paul Sartre, *La Critique de la Raison Dialectique*, Paris, 1957, Vol. I.
9. For some one, whose mother-tongue is not English, it is difficult to discern the meaning of 'freedom' from 'liberty.' (The same difficulty arises in Russian.) I can only feel that a difference in the scope of value-consciousness accounts for the difference in meaning of the two words. (Different is what *makes* a difference. C. S. Peirce)
10. This structuralistic approach is not so much indebted to Levi-Strauss ('Anthropologie Structurale') as it makes use of my own essay on '*Konkretisierbare Freiheit*', in *Kentaurische Philosophie*, Munich 1968.
11. *Cf.* George Herbert Mead, *Mind, Self and Reality*, and *The Social Act*.
12. *Cf.* Roderick, Seidenber. *Post-historic Man*, The University of North Carolina Press, 1950.

PART II

Automata, Purpose, and Value

LARRY HOLMES

State University of New York, College at New Paltz

I

The problem of the distinction between human beings and sophisticated machines of the robot sort has often been discussed in the context of whether robots can be made to exhibit characteristic behavior of humans or to accomplish all the 'mental' tasks that humans can (although not necessarily in the same way). Those who argue that there is at least one property or function of man that cannot be duplicated have chosen variously: some hold that language is the distinctive feature, others consciousness, emotion, or feelings, others the organic wholeness of man. Goal-seeking or purposive behavior was also one of the functions thought to be denied to automata. But this last position could not be maintained. The phenomena of negative feedback in organisms and machines have been explored sufficiently, I should suppose, to make clear that machines *can* be constructed capable of proceeding 'purposively' toward almost any given end, and even with the 'choice' of alternate means or the 'selection' of more effective means if one possibility is blocked or unsuccessful.

I wish to argue that there is, related to purposiveness, one area of essential difference between humans and automata that has not thus far been replicated or simulated, even 'in principle.' This is that automata cannot choose their own goals and values, cannot determine purposes, whereas humans can and do.[1] My fundamental premiss concerning these human abilities is neatly expressed by Ruth Macklin:

> We impute to human beings the ability to select goals, formulate
> purposes, and to act to realize these chosen aims in accordance with
> beliefs and attitudes. . . . Our expectations that people do act rationally
> and our belief that they ought to act in a rational manner are both

predicated on the essential assumption that persons formulate purposes and have goals in mind when they act.[2]

Some would probably agree that only humans have purposes in this
sense, but other writers seem willing to attribute them to machines
too.[3] I believe that when such imputations of autonomy of purpose or
goals in machines are made, key terms are used in senses critically different from the philosophical uses, and that claims for machine capabilities are exaggerated.[4] I have not yet discovered a design or program
which did not, when analyzed carefully, reduce to implanting in the
machine goals and purposes of the human designer. I shall henceforth
refer to this as the *derivative* sense of goal-setting or purposefulness.
Since the classic paper of Rosenblueth, Wiener, and Bigelow in 1943
it has been permissible in science to use 'purposive' to refer to goal-
seeking homeostatic processes resulting from negative feedback.[5] This
is *not* what I am speaking of. There is no question that machines are
capable of this much.

Thus I maintain (1) that those who believe that machines *can*
'entertain purposes' in a non-derivative, non-metaphorical sense should
exercise great care in making claims; (2) that the best way to answer the
question about such capabilities in machines would be, at minimum, to
design a program and specify machine characteristics which can stand
up under challenge; and (3), that (2) is unlikely until we have a better
analysis of the concept of human purpose than is now available.

II

Detailed analysis of the terms useful in discussion of topics of men and
machines would be highly desirable, but the great variation in usage
guarantees that the analysis would be a lengthy one. I shall merely indicate the scope within which I shall apply certain key terms.

I shall use 'automaton,' 'robot,' or 'machine' without strict differentiation. 'Machine' will be understood here to refer to complex,
sophisticated automata or robots or computers. 'Machine' comprehends
any such entity that is contrived, constructed, put together, by human
beings out of components that pre-exist separately from the machine as
a whole. We cannot beg questions by defining functionally, but let us
grant that the automaton can do whatever designers are capable of
making it do; not granting, however, mere assertions. Let us grant also

that its programming may be whatever the state of the designing art permits: as flexible and as advanced as possible.

It should be noted, though, that randomizing circuits, which are often asserted to enable a machine to be unpredictable to its designer, or to display 'originality,' do not solve the problem of autonomous purpose. It would appear, for one thing, that the range within which randomization works, or more exactly, what it is *for,* is set by the designer or programmer. More significantly, randomization conflicts with genuine purpose. Selection by this means—whether of an operation, an input, or an output—is not true *choice* at all, any more than it is when a man permits a decision to be made for him by tossing a coin, rather than deliberately choosing for himself. To be purposeful is to try one's best to *make* the outcome predictable, to strive to achieve a desired value. It has to do not only with the result, but with the way in which it is achieved. On can easily drop a ball into a hole; the game of golf, however, consists in doing it purposefully, by restricted means and according to certain rules. Even outside the realm of games, purposefulness is surely inconsistent with achievement of a goal by random guesses.

I do not believe it necessary to stipulate whether the components of the machine are to be inorganic, or may be organic. The stipulation that the machine be contrived by human or equivalent beings is necessary, though. If the entity were 'a natural organism (*e.g.,* a product of evolution),'[8] the philosophical questions might no longer be so interesting. We as conscious, value-creating, goal-formulating beings have arisen through evolution, so there is no reason why others should not.

When I use 'purpose,' I mean autonomous, deliberate purpose, initiated by the entity; and for 'goals,' genuine choice of goals, not just goal-seeking; and genuine positing of values, not just rating according to a given scale. Failure to distinguish these carefully from the derivative senses of purpose, goals, *etc.,* is responsible for many of the inflated claims for the capabilities of automata.

III

The philosopher delving into cybernetics must always risk the chilling rebuff that he simply does not know the field well enough to evaluate the claims made. But it is not presumptuous, surely, to expect cyberneticians, if their reasoning is mathematical, to justify its alleged correspondence with empirical and every-day concepts; and in their prose accounts, to use language precisely and non-animistically, if they would have us believe that the recognized accomplishments of automata actually manifest what they are said to manifest.

W. Mays in an early critique (which has not been heeded) called attention to the prevalence of psychological language (in the lay sense) in Turing's classic paper of 1950.[7] He quotes 'machines making decisions,' 'being punished and rewarded,' 'deliberately introducing mistakes,' 'doing homework.' It is natural to fall into this way of writing, but it has contributed greatly to the belief, among machine theorists as well as the lay public, that machines are in their capabilities closer to humans than is actually the case. The metaphorical or analogical extension of such terminology neglects the complex human context in which its meaningfulness has arisen. To be programmed to 'deliberately introduce a mistake,' for example, is quite different from making a mistake when one is trying his level best to be correct. A machine cannot, in the true sense of the term, make mistakes. (This is perhaps another of our distinctive characteristics, and a useful one.) The judgment of 'mistake' is one only we could make, if some process of the machine did not conform to our purpose. Mistakes involve intentions and purposes; in order to understand wrongly an entity first has to understand, and it has not been shown that machines can do this.

I can mention here only one sample of what I consider misleading claims. From the titles of some of the articles of Dr. Warren S. McCulloch, the well known neurologist and cybernetician, one is led to believe that machines have been developed which, presumably in the usual philosophical senses, deal with values and function ethically and purposefully. Here are titles from his book, *Embodiments of Mind*[8]: 'A Heterarchy of Values Determined by the Topology of Nervous Nets'; 'Toward Some Circuitry of Ethical Robots or an Observational Science of the Genesis of Social Evaluation in the Mind-Like Behavior of Artifacts'; 'Machines that Think and Want.' Others, less startling, make similar claims. I shall examine only the second of the three articles mentioned, because the principal message of the first article is recapitulated there, and the third one I do not discover to say anything at all about 'machines that want.'

Dr. McCulloch disarms some criticism by indicating that he is not speaking of a normative science of values, which he identifies with a tautological theory of the good, like mathematics or logic. The identification is questionable in itself, though, and one would suppose that for philosophers the normative area is where the real problem lies. He places his work in 'an observational science of evaluation.'[9]

McCulloch begins, as most of his articles in this area do, with a summary of the negative feedback mechanism as presented in the Rosenblueth, Wiener, and Bigelow paper on teleological mechanisms. This can alert us at once to the unlikelihood that the writer is going to understand purpose in anything other than the derivative sense. After a few sentences, he slips easily into personal pronouns: 'The mere fact that *his fellows* are appetitive, requires the machine to treat them as appetitive, even if *he* only *wants* to *use* them for *his own* ends.' (Emphasis supplied.)

McCulloch then summarizes his earlier paper on the value anomaly, or circularity of preference, in which a man or animal may prefer A to B, and B to C, but then prefer C to A. This, as he says, can easily be modelled in a circuit. He believes (and stresses elsewhere) that this shows that we cannot arrange ends or goals in a hierarchy of values, as some philosophers have tried to do. But although there may be an anomaly, it is one which indicates further problems, not a solution of a major value problem as he believes it to be. There is no question that this kind of modelling of descriptive value situations may be useful, but it does not show that value processes are going on in the machine, any more than diagramming geometrical figures shows that mathematical reasoning is going on in the diagrams. His 'heterarchy of values' shows that it is possible to model by electrical circuits a situation in which value judgments are not transitive. But it is also possible, surely, to model one in which they are. How can it manifest any more than this, save through animistic interpretation? To say, as he does, that 'a six-celled nervous system may be constructed as to enjoy no *summum bonum*' is to confuse the model with the thing modelled.

What, then, are his 'ethical robots'? He considers a universal Turing machine, say in the form of a chess-playing machine. A machine can be built whose subsequent operations depend upon the data made newly available to it from the environment or as the result of one of its own operations. This, he says, 'imports a capacity for inductive reasoning.' (I imagine a good many philosophers troubled by the problems of induction wish things were as easy as this.) It is, then, capable of picking up the rules of a game by playing, without the rules being programmed in advance. It is required only that the opponent will not play unless the machine 'abides by the rules'—in more neutral words, it has to keep making moves until it makes one which the opponent will respond to. McCulloch extrapolates this to the social, in a wonderfully animistic passage, in which I again stress the words which begin to persuade us to think of the computer as human: 'A machine who plays *spontaneously,* whenever *he finds* an opponent, must have a feedback circuit that makes *him want* to play, and once playing *he* must *attempt* to win. These characteristics *make* his behavior essentially social.' I need not belabor the obvious; in what other than an overly-extended metaphorical sense can a computer be said to do these things?

This kind of machine McCulloch calls ethical, because 'they are free in the sense that we, their creators, have neither told them what they ought to do, nor so made them that they cannot behave inappropriately. ... He can learn to play Go, or checkers, or any other game he finds the accepted mode of behavior in his society.' I submit that what he has described is not ethical behavior at all, in any usual sense. Behavior is not ethical because free; nor is it ethical because one has been told (or *not* told) what one ought to do. Inappropriate behavior is not necessarily unethical behavior; and many sorts of rule-following activities are not at all ethical.

Nor is it correct to say that we have not told the machines what they ought to do. His machine plays against another machine which *does* 'know what to do,' does 'know' the rules of a particular game because this information was programmed into it by a human who already knew the rules. Thus it is purposive, if at all, only in the derivative sense. If neither machine 'knew' the rules, if they both 'attempted freely' by 'induction' to guess the rules by trial and error, their operations would be futile, because there would not be anything there to guess. They would not be able to make up rules, to make up a game, as human do.

The best refutation there could be of my skepticism concerning machine capabilities would be for someone to construct, or at least show precisely how one could construct, an automaton with the required capabilities. It is only fair to say that there are some sober and promising accounts of interesting attempts to do this. Donald M. MacKay, for example, scrupulously avoids animistic belief or language. He writes in the terminology of modelling or simulating human mental processes, and with great philosophical insight. I cannot do justice to his approach here; he is well aware of the difficulties I am about to mention (in his terminology, the 'underspecified' nature of human activity), and is attempting to cope with these in his models by use of evaluative feedbacks to control probabilities of transitions to new states, and by setting up 'metaorganizational hierarchies' to correspond to the human ability to carry on a complexity of activities by organizing them into levels, higher levels integrating lower ones.[10] Yet even these models do not so far manifest anything approaching autonomous choice and purpose.

IV

One way that the charge that machines cannot be autonomously purposeful, and so on, has been met is the 'you're another' rejoinder. It may not have been possible, yet, to construct autonomously purposeful machines; but then, humans are not *really* autonomous in that line either. And if humans themselves are programmed, there is no reason to believe that a machine program cannot be devised to accomplish whatever humans accomplish. Paraphrasing Spinoza, it is said that humans just *think* they choose their own goals and initiate purposes to strive for them. Actually, God, the Great Programmer as well as Manufacturer, has designed our purposes into us.[11] Or, in the naturalist version, humans are said to be controlled and programmed by their structure and environment, and the various sorts of conditioning thereby provided.[12]

The first form of this counter-charge is not worth much attention. To say that the human situation is no different from that of our machines because perhaps God chooses our purposes for us, has at least two flaws: (1) It changes the game to another court, from purpose in the individual, goal-seeking and goal-positing sense to Teleology in the final cause sense, and from naturalism to supernaturalism. We speak slightingly of the *deus ex machina* as a type of explanation; can this use of the God-concept, a *deus pro machina,* be any less otiose? (2) It is questionable theology, in Christian belief at least, because it turns us from morally autonomous *persons* into mechanical toys of the Deity. Some have claimed that this is exactly what God has done, but it is surely not necessary to believe this, in the face of so much counter-evidence, religious and practical. (I find it a satisfactory answer to this ploy, too, to say that even if God does choose our purposes, He hasn't let us know clearly what they are, so we are still under the living necessity of choosing them ourselves.)

The other form of the response is more important, and not so easily dismissed. For some purposes, it *should* be maintained. Surely the scientific hypothesis that man has a 'program,' analogous to that of the computer, and that his behavior can be accounted for on the basis of his structure, this 'program,' and the input he receives, is a valuable one. It keeps open the road of inquiry, as Peirce says.

The well-known book by Miller, Galanter and Pribram, *Plans and the Structure of Behavior,* is, its authors say, an attempt to take this hypothesis seriously.[13] By 'plan' they mean man's 'organized set of instructions that he attempts to execute.' Their search for this is tremendously interesting and valuable, but in the end fruitless. As they admit at the end of the chapter on the neurological search for such a program and its origin, 'One of the most interesting aspects of brain function ... is how Plans are constructed in the first place, how they are formed.' One can only concur. But they go on to say, 'The present discussion has been confined to the more limited task of describing how Plans must be executed. ... The authors are not sure where or how the brain might generate Plans.'[14] Until we are sure, we can scarcely simulate such generation.

What, then, of this view? As Dennis Thompson puts it, just as 'everything the machine turns out is a result of its structure, its programme and stimulation, and the changes it makes in its programme,' so also 'everything a human produces is a result of his structure, the stimuli he receives, and what he does with what he has learned.'[15] This may be true enough, since it seems to include everything, but it does not tell us much. What we should like to know is *how* the human puts all these together, and whether what he does can be simulated or replicated in a machine.

And is it really the case, to narrow the issue a bit, that our goals are 'pre-set'?

One need not underestimate the extent to which the goals of humans *are* set by 'nature,' but neither need it be overestimated. For every basic natural goal, there have probably been humans who have shown their autonomy by taking its contrary as their goal. For example, basic biological goals are usually said to include food, reproduction, and survival. But the deliberate rejection of eating, in the age-old practice of fasting, has often been considered a high moral goal. Celibacy has also been taken as a value. As for survival, not only are there many goals for which men are willing to give up their lives, but in a society such as feudal Japan there were set occasions when suicide was expected, a social obligation. (Suicide was part of the way of life, you might say.) Even some of the homeostatic, self-regulatory activities of the body, of which we are for the most part unconscious, can be overridden by the human controller, in order to achieve other, deliberate goals (*e.g.,* in the practice of Yoga).

Nature does indeed suggest certain goals and purposes, sometimes rather forcefully. There may be severe penalties, even to extinction, for contravening them. There are, in A. R. Louch's useful expression, human 'paradigm aims.'[16] The larger of these result from, and emphasize, the fact that we share a common humanity in a common world. It is likely that the natural goals will be accepted, normally without our even thinking of them. But they *can* be rejected, autonomously, and have been.

The fact that most ordinary goals and values are acquired from our social environment does not mean, either, that those that come from society are not deliberate, not autonomous human purposes. The values of a society which are taught or even enforced upon an individual within it came originally from other men, established by them collectively or individually, not from some mysterious outside source. We have the power by becoming aware of the conditioning to overcome it.[17] The moral prophets are those who, refusing the value systems they find in society, have been able to establish new values.

(If no one is free to do more than react to his environment—which ordinarily is taken to mean to 'succumb to it,' to accept the given mode of behavior—we have what might be called the 'chain-letter fallacy.' Each person is said to get his values only from others. But where does it all come from, at last analysis? By what magic are we able, separately or collectively, to condition other individuals when we cannot as individuals condition ourselves?)

V

We may grant that any human behavior which can be explicitly described in a finite number of words, or even statistically can 'in principle' be replicated or simulated in a machine. This has not been notably successful with respect to human purposeful behavior, however.

It may be that the inability to design and program an autonomously purposeful, goal-choosing machine is a reflection of our lack of knowledge of what these processes are in ourselves. D. M. MacKay points out 'the *conceptual* difficulty (if not impossibility) for a human being to comprehend fully, and explicitly, what it is to be a human being.'[18] As M. Polanyi has put it, 'we can know more than we can tell.'[19] And if we cannot tell it, we cannot very well program it for a machine.

One dislikes saying that a process we carry on all the time is mysterious, but the best efforts to elucidate the concept of purpose have not given us much light. Nor has a convincing non-teleological account of human behavior been given, as Charles Taylor, for one, has shown.[20]

One reason for the difficulty in analysis could be that given by Richard Taylor, in his book *Action and Purpose* and his article, 'Thought and Purpose.'[21] He believes that purpose is a basic category; hence it can be the foundation of certain kinds of explanation, but is not itself further analyzable, nor further subject to explanation. There may be merit in his suggestion. He has made a persuasive case (complemented by Charles Taylor's approach) that it is more satisfactory to use purpose to explain behavior than to use behavior to explain purpose.

That an attempt to give a programmatic description of purpose is fundamentally mistaken is suggested also by A. R. Louch, who holds that purposes are not behavioral events at all:

> Recognizing or comprehending purposes is not a matter of observing particular events or successions of them. It is rather a matter of setting what a man or animal is doing in a context that makes those movements intelligible. It is seeing that a bodily movement is consistent with or, more strongly, logically entails, a consequence which, in its turn, can be seen as something worthy of being attained.[22]

Keith Gunderson has suggested something similar in labelling certain aspects of mentality, such as having pains, emotions, *etc.*, 'program-resistant,' in comparison with the problem-solving type of activity reasonably successfully simulated on computers. They 'are not potentially well-defined tasks which hence may be programmable, for they are not tasks at all. . . . They are not the sorts of things which a robot could do. They may be had, but not done.'[23]

Polanyi reminds us that Kant, trying to determine the rules of pure reason, had to admit that no system of rules could prescribe the procedure by which the rules themselves are to be applied; and no more, I would add, are we likely to be able to prescribe the procedure by which the rules are chosen.[24] If this is the case, that we reach a level at which one can no longer give specifications in the form of rules, but must attempt to account for the holding of the rules (which may in turn be supposed to be on the basis of values sought), then it will be difficult, if not impossible, to simulate the process by machine.

VI

There has been considerable philosophical interest in our potential relations with automata. It has been said, for example, that we may have to determine whether to treat them as fellow members of our linguistic community, or whether they are to be considered as persons, perhaps because they are conscious, or have feelings like ourselves. If these questions were to become truly live issues, we would also have to settle the problem of our moral relations with robots. Whatever we might be inclined to decide about the admission of robots to our *linguistic* community, we would not wish to consider them members of our *moral* community unless it could be shown that they hold value systems in the same sense we do, and that as a specific indication of this, they could formulate, accept, or reject such systems, including the concomitant purposes and goals, and behave accordingly. *Community* connotes a sharing and participation, so that a decision of ours to *treat* robots as moral beings, along the lines of Hilary Putnam's suggestion that it is up to us to decide whether to include them in the linguistic community,[25] would be mere sentimentalism unless they were capable of reciprocating, and sharing values.

It is highly doubtful, however, that machines could be constructed that would be able to do this. It is difficult to see in what sense the machine could be considered to be moral or immoral; it simply is. It has not been shown that the machine chooses or rejects or fails to choose goals; it simply does nothing until a goal is inserted. There is no evidence that the machine is either disappointed at failing to reach the goal set for it, or elated at reaching it; it simply turns off, or prints out 'Q.E.D.' The machine does not value or disvalue; it can simply rate presented input on the basis of programmed value scales. The machine has no values; it simply has value for us. As appears to be the case also with animals, we might very well consider that there are moral implications in our treatment of machines, but this is derivative from our own value system, not from theirs, since there is no reason to believe that they have one.

Thus if we can attribute genuine autonomous purpose and the holding of value systems neither to animals nor machines, we appear to be alone in having them.

VII

The failure of absolutism in values has sometimes been regarded as a catastrophe for rational moral life. I have here stressed as a distinctive, possibly unique, characteristic of man his ability to establish value systems, and to formulate, within the reasonably wide parameters of the conditions of life, his own goals and purposes. Grace de Laguna points out 'the profound influence of man's purposeful activities in the course of organic evolution. . . . To an increasing extent he has substituted his own 'selection' for that of nature. Although he is in himself the product of the 'blind' forces of nature, he has, for the first time, introduced purposes into the course of nature.'[26] Value is implicit in the relations of an organism to its environment; only in man is value made explicit.

Do we really need an extra-human, absolute support for values? A recognized absolute value system would in fact place our freedom in question. For it could scarcely be gainsaid; we would have to hold to it. But our characteristic autonomy of purpose, involving also an autonomy of value, can be a challenge and an enhancement of human life, rather than a cause for gloomy fears of moral anarchy. It may not be a bad thing that we must 'do it ourselves,' that we are clearly responsible to ourselves for what we do, with no possibility of shifting the blame. If we but use our opportunities wisely, they give us the chance to make and remake our world, including human life itself. Where other animals must accept the lot given them by nature, and live within the rigid boundaries of their instinctive 'programmed' behavior, we have the awesome but at the same time glorious chance to *choose* our behavior, choose our values and goals, and the freedom to modify ourselves, our tools and the world to achieve these values. In so doing, automata will be of material assistance, but they can scarcely take over the task for us. I cannot pound nails with my hand, but because I use a hammer to do what I cannot do for myself, the hammer does not become human, nor I any less a man for using it. Autonomy in these matters, for better or worse, is ours and—as far as we can see now—no one else's.

Acknowledgement

Research from which this article developed was aided materially by a Faculty Research Fellowship and Grant-in-Aid from the Research Foundation of State University of New York.

Notes and References

1. I shall not discuss one of the most popular topics in this field, namely whether machines can be conscious, because I do not think it is material to the limited issue I want to raise. I do not see how an entity can have the goal-formulating, value-setting characteristics specified without being conscious, but if this

should prove incorrect, one could still ask whether machines of any kind could have the characteristics in question here.

2. Ruth Macklin, 'Norm and Law in the Theory of Action,' *Inquiry*, **11** (Winter, 1968), pp. 407–408.

3. C. J. Ducasse comments:

A servo-mechanism, no matter how elaborate, is still a mechanism only. It may have been constructed by a *purposive being p* for the purpose of providing the eventual *users* of it with a mechanism that will enable them to achieve automatically certain of *their* purposes. But the servo-mechanism does not itself *entertain a purpose* in the sense in which its constructor did and its users do.

(In J. R. Smythies, ed., *Brain and Mind*, New York: Humanities Press, 1965, p. 234.)

Among those who agree with this point of view are Antony Flew, 'A Rational Animal,' in Smythies, *op. cit.*, p. 112; Rolf Gruner, 'Teleological and Functional Explanation,' *Mind*, **75** (1966), pp. 516–517; R. Thomson and W. Sluckin, 'Cybernetics and Mental Functioning,' *British Journal for the Philosophy of Science*, **IV** (August 1953), pp. 138–143; W. Sluckin, *Minds and Machines* (Baltimore: Penguin Books, rev. ed., 1960), pp. 213–214.

Among those who, in one way or another, go farther than I consider justified in attributing purpose, intentionality, goal-setting, *etc.*, to machines (at least 'in principle') are Margaret A. Boden, 'Machine Perception,' *The Philosophical Quarterly*, **19** (January 1969), pp. 33–45 (see especially p. 44, where she refers, as if it were about to be accomplished in machines, to 'the autonomous selection of goals'); Peter J. Manicas, 'Men, Machines, Materialism, and Morality,' *Philosophy and Phenomenological Research*, **XXVII** (December 1966), especially pp. 243–245; Michael A. Simon, 'Could There be a Conscious Automaton?,' *American Philosophical Quarterly*, **VI** (January 1969), pp. 71–78; J. J. C. Smart, *Philosophy and Scientific Realism* (London: Routledge & Kegan Paul, 1963), Chapter VI; and, implicitly at least, Hilary Putnam, in 'Robots: Machines or Artificially Created Life?,' *Journal of Philosophy*, **61** (1964), pp. 668–691, and 'The Mental Life of Some Machines,' in H. N. Castañeda, ed., *Intentionality, Minds and Perception* (Detroit: Wayne State University Press, 1967), pp. 177–200.

4. Seeing the title of J. A. Deutsch's article 'A Machine with Insight' (*Quarterly Journal of Experimental Psychology*, **6**, 1954), for example, one hopes to find some machine assistance for the pressing problems we seek insight into; but the machine, however creditably, simply can learn two mazes, and take advantage of short-cuts *when such are introduced*. (Described in W. Sluckin, *Minds and Machines*, p. 67.) And Margaret A. Boden (*op. cit.*, p. 39) takes at face value the title of a program developed by L. Uhr and C. Vossler, 'A Pattern Recognition Program that Generates, Evaluates, and Adjusts its own Operators" (reprinted in E. A. Feigenbaum and J. Feldman, eds., *Computers and Thought;* New York: McGraw-Hill, 1963, pp. 251–268), although I believe a careful reading of the article will show that these things are done only in a derivative sense, with the operators and evaluating criteria inserted by the programmer.

5. Arturo Rosenblueth, Norbert Wiener, and Julian Bigelow, 'Behavior. Purpose, and Teleology,' *Philosophy of Science*, **X** (January 1943), pp. 18–24,

Reprinted in John V. Canfield, ed., *Purpose in Nature* (Englewood Cliffs, N.J.: Prentice-Hall, 1966), pp. 9–16.

6. Denis Thompson, 'Can a Machine be Conscious?,' *British Journal for the Philosophy of Science*, **XVI** (May 1965), p. 34n.

7. W. Mays, 'Can Machines Think?,' *Philosophy*, **XXVII** (April 1952), pp. 152–153. Reference is to A. M. Turing, 'Computing Machines and Intelligence,' *Mind*, **LIX** (1950), reprinted in Alan Ross Anderson, *Minds and Machines* (Englewood Cliffs, N.J.: Prentice-Hall, 1964), pp. 4–30.

8. Warren S. McCulloch, *Embodiments of Mind* (Cambridge: M.I.T. Press 1965).

9. *Ibid*, p. 196. Quotations in remaining comments on the McCulloch article are from pp. 196–199.

10. From Dr. MacKay's long list of publications, I can mention only a few which are closest to the present topic: 'Cerebral Organization and the Conscious Control of Action,' in *The Brain and Conscious Experience*, J. R. Eccles, ed., (New York: Springer-Verlag, 1966), pp. 422–445 (from a conference at Vatican City; page numbers include the discussion); 'From Mechanism to Mind', in Smythies, *op. cit.*, pp. 163–191; 'The Use of Behavioral Language to refer to Mechanical Processes,' *British Journal for the Philosophy of Science*, **XIII** (August 1950), pp. 89–103; 'Mindlike Behavior in Artefacts,' *ibid.*, **II** (1951), pp. 105–121.

11. As in A. R. Lacey, 'Men and Robots,' *The Philosophical Quarterly*, **10** (January 1960), p. 61; and J. J. C. Smart, 'Professor Ziff on Robots,' *Analysis*, **XIX** (1959), reprinted in A. R. Anderson, *Minds and Machines*, pp. 104–105.

12. See, for example, Roland Puccetti, 'On Thinking Machines and Feeling Machines,' *British Journal for the Philosophy of Science*, **XVIII** (1967), p. 41; and Thomas S. Szasz, 'Men and Machines,' *ibid.*, **VIII** (1958), pp. 310–317.

13. George A. Miller, Eugene Galanter, and Karl H. Pribram, *Plans and the Structure of Behavior* (New York: Henry Holt, 1968), pp. 197–198.

14. *Ibid.*, p. 208.

15. Thompson, *op. cit.*, p. 36.

16. A. R. Louch, *Explanation and Human Action* (Oxford: Basil Blackwell, 1966), p. 123.

17. Grace A. de Laguna holds a similar view:
'While man is in some sense pre-adapted to culture, the teleonomic structure essential to a human "way of life" is not itself congenital. What is inherited is only a general and plastic capacity for it. . . .

There is no single end to which man is distinctively directed comparable to the supreme end of reproduction for which the biological creature is organized. The particular culture in which an individual is reared makes some ends possible to him and fails to provide opportunities for other ends possible in another culture. . . . Man must in some degree determine his own ends, and in his human freedom 'make his own life'.

('The Role of Teleonomy in Evolution,' *Philosophy of Science*, **29**, April 1962, pp. 130–131.)

18. D. M. MacKay, 'From Mechanism to Mind,' in Smythies, *op. cit.*, p. 198. See also p. 185.

19. Michael Polanyi, *The Tacit Dimension* (Garden City, N.Y.: Doubleday, 1967), p. 4.

20. Charles Taylor, *The Explanation of Behaviour* (London: Routledge and Kegan Paul, 1964).

21. Richard Taylor, *Action and Purpose* (Englewood Cliffs: Prentice-Hall, 1966); 'Thought and Purpose,' *Inquiry* 12 (Summer, 1969), pp. 149–169.

22. Louch, *op. cit.*, pp. 120–121.

23. Keith Gunderson, 'Robots, Consciousness, and Programmed Behavior,' *British Journal for the Philosophy of Science*, **XIX** (1968), p. 115. Ulric Neisser, too, has pointed out some of the deep differences in the thinking of men and of machines, in 'The Imitation of Man by Machine,' *Science*, **139** (18 January 1963), pp. 193–197.

24. Michael Polanyi, 'Experience and the Perception of Pattern,' in Kenneth M. Sayre and Frederick J. Crosson, eds., *The Modeling of Mind* (Notre Dame: University of Notre Dame Press, 1963), p. 207.

25. Hillary Putnam, 'Robots: Machines or Artificially Created Life?,' *Journal of Philosophy*, **61** (1964), p. 690.

26. De Laguna, *op. cit.*, p. 125.

Hegel and Hypnosis: Psychological Science and The Spirit

MURRAY GREENE

New School for Social Research

In Thomas Mann's story *Mario and the Magician,* a youthful onlooker at a magical performance is called up to the stage and made to kiss the puckered lips of the triumphant magician. The latter, a deformed but compelling magnetizer, has bewitched the youth into taking his repulsive countenance for the face of the youth's beloved. The shudder of revulsion that passes through the reader is precisely the effect sought by the author, who has skillfully associated the happening on the stage with the condition of dictatorship in Mussolini's Italy. What is this strange power of one human being over another, the reader wonders, that can have such fateful results for the political community? Mann the artist is not burdened with explaining hypnosis scientifically. His is not the problem of showing how a psychological understanding of the phenomenon might also help explain our esthetic reaction to it, or why the shocking 'magical' trick could serve as a political paradigm.

That man's physical life is of decisive importance for the life of the polity was long ago recognized by Plato, whose account of the soul of the tyrant, for example, is justly celebrated. Hegel, like Plato and Mann, views the psychical life in its potentialities for freedom and unfreedom, good and evil. Hegel's treatment seeks to demonstrate these potentialities scientifically, the scientific account at the same time remaining essentially one with the moral judgment. In this he is like Plato, whose analysis of the tyrant's soul as dominated by what tends toward non-being is one with the judgment that that soul is evil. Where Plato deals with orders of Being, however, Hegel deals with forms of spirit, whose order is established according to determinations of the Idea. Hegel seeks to unite his psychological explanation of hypnosis and his moral judgment upon it by means of his science of spirit, and of the psyche and consciousness as determinate phases of spirit.

The phenomenon of hypnosis, according to Hegel, reveals in rather startling fashion the nature and potentialities of the psyche as spirit.[1] For Hegel, as for Thomas Mann, the relation of two individuals in the hypnotic trance has a degrading aspect. The trance, for Hegel, is in fact a regression (*Herabsinken*) from a higher to a lower level of spirit: and the term 'regression,' as we shall see, has for Hegel both explanatory and axiological force. But at the same time that hypnosis is a regression of spirit, Hegel views the phenomena of the trance as manifesting the possibility in the psyche for the highest kinds of spirituality. But how can it show the psyche to have this opposite-sided character?

Even in the story *Mario and the Magician* we can to some extent see why the psyche must be a capacity for opposites. If, as the story shows us, there is the possibility in the psyche for the bondage of dictatorship, must it not also be a possibility for the bond of community? In making Mario kiss him, is not the magician drawing upon that same power that makes possible Mario's tie to his sweetheart? In Hegel's notion of the psyche as a form of spirit, hypnosis is viewed as a debased manifestation of the universal *philia* without which human community could not be a spiritual community. But spirit for Hegel is subjectivity. The scientific view of hypnosis sees it in terms of the nature and development of subjectivity.

I

At the opening of his Philosophy of Spirit, Hegel points excitedly to what he regards as new evidence for the existence of a psychical subjectivity prior to the level of the objective consciousness. Hegel terms this preobjective subjectivity 'soul' (*Seele*), and the new evidence, he claims, confirms his speculative notion of the nature of the soul as spirit.

> The substantial unity of the soul, and its power of ideality have recently been brought before the very gaze of experience by the phenomena of animal magnetism, which have thrown into confusion all the rigid distinctions of Understanding and have shown the direct necessity of a speculative approach to the problems of the soul.[2]

Part of Hegel's excitement about 'animal magnetism' was that he believed the new phenomena indicated a level of subjectivity prior to the 'I think' of the objective consciousness. This would support his criticism of Kant as having dealt with only one level of mind, namely, consciousness.[3] But consciousness, Hegel now claims to show, first 'awakens' in the soul; ego and the subject-object relation first 'emerge' from the preobjective psychical life. This would indicate, Hegel believed, that mind is more than consciousness; and the preobjective level of mind shows us something of the essence of the ego, which Kant maintained was hidden from our theoretical knowledge. It is to this preobjective level that the subjectivity of consciousness regresses in the hypnotic trance. But to speak of regression implies a concept of advance, and it is in the context of the development of the soul to ego that Hegel explains hypnosis as a regression.

The advance of the soul to the ego of consciousness, according to Hegel, is an ascension in ideality: that is to say, a development in determinateness of the Idea. On this sort of scale alone—with regard only to this kind of ascension—can we speak philosophically of advance or regression, as far as Hegel is concerned. The ascension in ideality is marked by a movement of the categories of the Logic and hence indicates an ascension in Being, since the Science of Logic is also the Hegelian ontology. Every advance is in an unfolding of the Idea, such an unfolding consisting at once in an externalization and an interealization, a going outward and a going inward, or, as Hegel puts it, a 'greater extension' that is also 'higher intensity.'[4] The only such advance we need note in the Logic is that from Being to Essence. This purely logical advance has its corresponding movement in the realm of concrete spirit in the advance from soul to consciousness; and this is our area of concern. Essence, for Hegel, is the sphere of 'reflectedness': Essence is Being 'coming into mediation with itself through the negativity of itself.'[5] In the same way, the subjectivity of consciousness is a self-reflectedness in other; it is a relation to self in the form of a relation to the object as the 'other' or negative of the self.[6] As such a reflectedness of self in other—or 'mediated' self-relation—consciousness constitutes an advance over soul, which, as we shall shortly note, is an 'immediate' or monadic inner self-relation. All advance or regression in the realm of nature or spirit is according to the scale of the ideal order of the categories of the Logic. In the Philosophy of Nature, for example, organism is an advance over mechanism; and in certain sickness states, where there is an obstruction in the fluid life of the organism, we may speak of a regression to mechanism.[7]

The emergence of the soul from nature is such an ascension in ideality, according to Hegel, since the soul is a form of spirit proper, and the development of nature is toward its 'truth' as spirit. The emergence of the soul marks nature's self-overcoming as a Being-outside-self (*Aussersichsein*), a realm of the *partes extra partes,* the 'this-beside-this' (*dieses neben diesem*).[8] Every step in this movement, *e.g.* from chemism to organism, and from one step to another within organism, has been an ascension in ideality, a simultanous going outward and going inward. This movement does not cease with the emergence of soul.

The soul, according to Hegel, is spirit still immersed in naturalness, namely, its own corporeality, the determinations of sensation and feeling. But the soul is also subjectivity; and on this level of spirit, according to Hegel, subjectivity is but 'inner' or 'monadic' subjectivity. In the ongoing development of spirit, the monadic subjectivity develops to the ego of consciousness. But even this is not the end of the ascension in ideality. As a consciousness and self-consciousness, the particular subjectivity determines itself to a universal or 'we' self-consciousness, as in the ethical community, which proceed to yet higher forms of spiritual life. There is thus one line of development from the psychical life of the monadic subjectivity to the highest forms of spirituality.

For our particular purposes, however, there is an important difference between the purely formal advance of the logical categories and the advance in the realm of concrete spirit, which includes the various stages of finite subjectivity. In the latter realm there is possible an *Herabsinken* on the part of particular subjectivities, as in certain forms of mental illness. Hypnosis, for Hegel, is for the patient a regression from the level of the waking objective consciousness to the pre-objective somnambulistic subjectivity. To explain hypnosis as a regression we must therefore understand the advance from the preobjective subjectivity to the ego of consciousness.

II

On the level of consciousness, according to Hegel, we distinguish ourselves from the objective outer world, to which at the same time we relate ourselves in the various modes of objective knowing.[9] As soul, or subjectivity prior to consciousness, however, the self is 'wrapped up' within itself as an inner world of feeling. The soul, says Hegel, is a monadic subjectivity, which does not relate itself to its manifold as to an objective outer world.[10] Its content comes to it as a dream world over which it is not yet itself the active power.

But as spirit, this monadic subjectivity is destined to become the active power over its feeling-life. With each step in the soul's development it becomes more truly a subjectivity, more truly the ideal unity of its feeling-manifold. These main steps, according to Hegel, are sensation (*Empfindung*), feeling (*Gefühl*), and habit (*Gewohnheit*). In habit, where the psychical subjectivity has mastered its feeling-life and rendered its corporeality an instrument of its will and purpose, the soul has actualized itself: it has attained the strength and self-possession to 'let go' its monadic feeling-manifold, which in this way is allowed to take on the form of an objective outer world opposite the subjectivity.[11] The coming into being of the objective outer world is thus simultaneous with the emergence of the ego of consciousness. Indeed, ego and objective world are but aspects—or perhaps better, resultants—of the same process. The positing of the inner content as external means in effect that the subjectivity has divided itself from its inner feeling-life. With the coming into being of the ego, the psychical subjectivity is sublated (*aufgehoben*) to a 'moment' of the objective consciousness. It no longer has a 'being-there' in consciousness as a separate subjectivity, but at the same time it has not disappeared. It manifests itself as the individual's inner demon or genius, which makes itself felt behind the scenes even through the waking consciousness;[12] it is also, what Hegel calls, the 'unconscious pit' (*bewusstlose Schlacht*) of the selfhood, the storehouse in which memories and experiences are deposited so that they never wholly disappear.[13]

The objective consciousness, according to Hegel, is a higher form of spirit than the psychical subjectivity. The content 'let go' to form a rationally structured outer world is a more highly idealized unity of a manifold than the more or less contingent dream associations of the monadic selfhood. But while the objective consciousness thus represents an ascension in ideality, and hence a higher form of spirit, its coming into being has meant a sunderance of the self as subjectivity from itself as a natural feeling-life. Ever underlying the objective consciousness of the finite selfhood, therefore, is that original schism of self out of which the ego emerged in the first place. For Hegel, the emergence of the objective consciousness signifies a great triumph of spirit in its movement toward rational subjectivity and moral reason. But for the finite individual, the price of this triumph is the ever-present possibility of an *Herabsinken,* as in the case of mental breakdown.

The concept of mental illness, says Hegel, has just as necessary a place in the science of subjective spirit as that of crime in the science of right.[14] This does not mean, Hegel says, that we must all go through mental breakdowns, any more than that we must go through a phase of criminality. It means that in mental health, as in a sound moral will, there is an ever-present exertion of the power of spirit as ideal unity of its manifold. In the same way, our standing erect—however unaware we may be of the effort—requires a constant exertion, without which we would instantly collapse in a heap. Hysteria, trance states, ecstasies, and certain forms of mental illness are viewed by Hegel as a giving up of the upright stance and clear-eyed attitude of the objective consciousness for the passive, inwardly rolling gaze of the oracle priestess.

Hegel views hypnosis as one such form of *Herabsinken* and thus a kind of sickness state. In the hypnotic trance, according to Hegel, there is a giving up of the objective consciousness by the patient, a surrendering of that consciousness which holds itself in erect and open-eyed confrontation of the world as an objective 'other.' Such a surrendering, Hegel points out, also occurs in healthy sleep, where the selfhood returns from the dispersal and distractions of waking life to the natural feeling-unity with itself. But the situation is not the same in the hypnotic trance. In the trance, says Hegel, the subjectivity of the patient is 'vibrated' or 'thrilled through' (*durchzittert*) by the subjectivity of an other.[15] The patient surrenders to the hypnotist his own relation as an independent ego to the external world. To be sure in the ordinary waking life of the self-possessed ego, independence is ofttimes given up, as demanded by social roles or in the name of a common task. Here, however, the relation of the subjectivities is a 'mediated' one. But in the trance, according to Hegel, the hypnotist and patient are in an 'immediate' relation. The subjectivity of the hypnotist is directly the ideal power over the feeling-life of the patient. The patient, says Hegel, hears, feels, sees 'in' the hypnotist.[16] This unity of subjectivities on the level of feeling is termed by Hegel a 'living-with-one-another' (*Ineinanderleben*), and a 'unity of souls' (*Seeleneinheit*). It is as such as *Ineinanderleben* that Hegel finds hypnosis so interesting philosophically. As an empirical phenomenon, hypnosis in the first place dramatically reveals the power of spirit as the overcoming of the 'this-beside-this' of the physical realm. As a regression, hypnosis reveals the nature of the psyche as a *dunamis ton enantion*. Finally, as a phenomenon we can study almost under experimental conditions, hypnosis, Hegel suggests, can give us an inkling, in the psychological realm, of what Hegel holds to be the deepest philosophical truth: the identity of substance and subject.[17]

On the level of soul, the identity of substance and subject revealed by hypnosis and other trance states is the identity of the inner world of feeling as permeated by the monadic subjectivity in the modes of dream and presentiment (*Durchtraumen und Ahnen*).[18] This world of feeling is in fact the soul's substantial being. I includes not only the complement of natural faculties, temperament, ethnic traits, *etc.*, possessed by the individual as a natural heritage, but also his deep-rooted ties to others that have sprung up in his experience and become interwoven with his inner being. As an actual individual, says Hegel, I am within myself a world of concrete content with an 'infinite periphery,'[19] a little universe of interconnections that grow and alter within me even without my explicit knowledge. This inner world is the individual's flesh and blood reality, the soul's home soil and ground, without which it cannot live as this particularity. This riches of content comprising the inner feeling-world of the individual is a manifold *vis-à-vis* the soul's simple unity. But the manifold and the unity are here nothing apart from one another: the feeling-life comprises the soul's concrete being and substance, which the psychical subjectivity knows as a dream world passing before its ken. Despite its fragmented character, says Hegel, the dream content is not merely contingent. Often the soul in dreams attains to 'a deep and powerful feeling of its entire individual nature,' the compass of its past, present, and future.[20]

This unity of the psychical subjectivity and its substantiality as actualized in dream and presentiment is nevertheless but an abstract and immediate unity. The subjectivity is passive; it does not yet have itself firmly 'in possession' in its manifold. As spirit, this merely 'formal' subjectivity is destined to actualize itself as the ego of consciousness, which will then contain the psychical subjectivity as but a sublated moment of itself. But in a regression from the objective consciousness to the psychical level, the *Aussereinandersein* of nature can once more display itself in the phenomenon of two subjectivities within the same self, the one the controlling power over the other. The anthropological basis for this *Ineinanderleben* is seen by Hegel in the relation of foetus and mother.[21]

In the foetus-mother relation, according to Hegel, the Being-for-self (*Fürsichsein*), or subjectivity, of the individual soul (of the foetus) and its Being-in-self (*Ansichsein*), or substantiality, are divided between two individuals in a *Seeleneinheit*. The soul of the foetus, says Hegel, cannot yet 'bear itself'; it can be 'for itself' only through another subjectivity. The Being-for-self of the foetus is 'born' by the subjectivity of the mother, to whose power the foetus lies 'wholly open.' The foetus is 'thrilled through' by the infusing 'genius' of the mother, which is thus the single self of both.

Hegel places considerable emphasis on this 'unity of souls' which he claims is the essential feature in the foetus-mother relationship. It is just such a 'unity of the distinguished,' says Hegel, that constitutes the very essence of spirit. Such a unity is incomprehensible to *Verstand,* which clings to the view that what is spatially and materially distinct must be absolutely distinct. To be sure, the foetus-mother relation has its merely natural side. But to take this relation as but a relation between organisms linked by physical connections, says Hegel, is to miss the essence of the matter: the 'immediate action' (*unmittelbares Einwirken*) that comprises the true nature of the foetus-mother *Ineinanderleben.*

The relation of substance and subject on the level of soul is most fully realized in the form of the individual's particular genius, according to Hegel.[22] The genius of the individual is the individual in his inner particularity, that which marks him off from a hundred other men in a given situation. I am a 'twofold being,' says Hegel. I am in the first place as I know myself in my everyday life and as I am known to my fellows. But I am also an 'inner' being with a certain special character that brings itself to bear on all my outer activities. This inner being, says Hegel, can be termed my 'fate,' my innner oracle, my *daimonion.* It is that 'intensive form of individuality' that often has the last word in my decisions, however handy I may be with 'reasons.' In its enveloping simplicity, says Hegel, the inner genius remains the kernel of the individual's feeling-selfhood, absorbing into itself the ties and connections of deepest moment to the individual. At the same time it remains distinct from the conscious selfhood as objectively reflected in the individual's social activities and relationships.

The individual's inner genius remains normally but a 'moment' of his active conscious life. As the inner voice behind the show of conscious intentions, the genius tends to direct the individual along subjective and particular lines, rather than in accordance with objective and universal requirements. Hence the present level of the psychical life is viewed by Hegel as ruled by capriciously subjective considerations; it is a realm of darkness rather than a great source of truth. The psychical subjectivity is normally *aufgehoben* as a moment of the objective rational consciousness, which thus becomes the proper guiding genius of the psychical life.

III

The rational consciousness, however, does not always retain its self-possession and mastery of the psychical life. When the rational self-hood abdicates its sovereignty, as in certain trance or sickness states, there is a regression to the level of the psychical life and the emergence once again of the psychical subjectivity as a power in its own right. In such abnormal states the monadic feeling-soul comes forth as a 'real' subjectivity. At this time the self is no longer in open-eyed encounter with an objective outer world but has become a somnambulistic, inwardly turned consciousness. The individual's inner genius, says Hegel, becomes a clairvoyant (*hellsehende*) subjectivity.[23] The self-possessed consciousness having retired before the passive feeling-selfhood, the individual now 'lies open' to the subjectivity of another as his controlling genius.

As a somnambulistic, clairvoyant subjectivity, says Hegel, the inwardly turned individual is in 'immediate' relation with his substantial being: the circle of his feeling-world comprising his deepest ties and interests, his family, his loyalties and attachments to home, soil, and community. The clairvoyant, says Hegel, is able to read off—as in a kind of 'gazing-knowing' (*schauendes Wissen*)—this content that has grown together with his inner life and substance. This same content on the level of objective consciousness can only be known 'mediately,' *i.e.* through causal inferences and the connecting of appearance according to the objective categories of the understanding.

Since the monadic subjectivity lacks that active distinguishing of consciousness in the subject-object relation, the self in the feeling-life is essentially passive. In somnambulism, cataleptic seizures, trances, forms of ecstasy, the self is 'possessed,' borne alone as by some inner demon dictating its doings and utterances, which thus emerge as automatic. In addition to this aspect of the self's passivity, the forms of 'gazing-knowing' also manifest a loss of articulateness and differentiation of content, as compared with objective knowing. Since the sickness states represent a withdrawal from the external world in all its manifold expansion, there is a reorienting of the modes of perceiving. The outwardly directed senses are dimmed as in sleep; their specificity is blurred, and their functions tend to become fused. The particular roles of the outer senses, Hegel claims, are taken over by a 'common-feeling' (*Gemeingefühl*) located in the self's more primitive digestive system.[24]

However dubitable may be Hegel's particular facts about somnambulistic or clairvoyant forms of knowing, his view implies that our everyday 'mediated' perceiving—*i.e.* mediated by objective structures of consciousness—involves a certain psychical health and attainment. Kant had already pointed out that objective experience in a logical sense required a spontaneous act of unity of the ego. Hegel now indicates that objectivity also requires a certain psychical development, where the self has become strong enough as a subjectivity to maintain a posture of objective disinterestedness. If we compare the character of 'gazing-knowing' with the mediated knowing of objective consciousness, we again see the meaning of the ascension in ideality from soul to ego: from the undifferentiatedness, inarticulatedness, and often vagueness of the psychical content, to the rationally structured, articulated objective content on the level of consciousness. The 'going outwards' that constitutes the emergence of an objective order is at the same time a 'going inwards' in the sense of an enrichment of meanings in a differentiated context. At the same time, Hegel makes much of the phenomena of somnambulistic knowing and clairvoyance, which, he says, can never be understood 'so long as we assume independent personalities, independent of one another and of the objective world which is their content—so long as we assume the absolute spatial and material externality of one part of being to another.'[25]

That the original feeling-unity of the psychical life is prior to the subject-object antithesis in consciousness is nowhere more strikingly evident than in the hypnotic trance, according to Hegel. Here, in Hegel's view, we are able to witness an artificially induced regression from the objective consciousness to the psychical feeling-life, from the active to the passive selfhood, from independence to dependence. The psychical subjectivity to which the patient retires in the hypnotic trance, according to Hegel, is a subjectivity that has not yet established itself as the unifying power and master of its feeling-manifold. For this reason, says Hegel, the subjectivity of the patient 'lies open' before the infusing genius of the hypnotist like the foetus in the womb.[26]

The foetus-mother *Ineinanderleben* is viewed by Hegel as a kind of prototypical psychical unity of two subjectivities.[27] The hypnotist-patient relation in the trance, as well as certain morbid personal relationships, have the aspect of a regression to the foetus-mother relation, and Hegel notes instances of such relations in history and literature. A psychical unity of two adults, such as in the hypnotic trance, can mean a surrender of the free rational consciousness on the part of one and a morbid exercise of power on the part of the other. A well-known example in literature would be the relationship between Uriah Heep and Mr. Wickfield, which surely evokes in the reader a similar revulsion and uneasiness to that in the instance of Mario's kissing the magician.

<h1 style="text-align:center">IV</h1>

Between master and slave, Aristotle tells us, there can be no justice or injustice. These relations can exist only between those 'who share equally in ruling and being ruled.'[28] In our discussion thus far, we have been considering whether there is an important psychological dimension in such sharing. The relation of master and slave is not between equals but rather, according to Aristotle, like that of whole and part. In his discussion of hypnosis and forms of the *Ineinander-leben* of two adults, Hegel shows the possibility of a psychological master-slave relation where the latter is psychologically a 'part' of the former. Mario, Hegel would say, is 'thrilled through' by the magnetizer's subjectivity—which is here the infusing whole, of which Mario has been reduced to a non-independent part.[29]

This kind of master-slave *Ineinanderleben,* though a form of regression, shows the inherent ideality of spirit as identity of the distinct and the inner truth of the 'this-beside-this' of the nonspiritual realm. But the characteristic inwardness of spirit is exhibited not in its forms of regression, but more truly in its advance to higher forms of ideality. In ethical love, according to Hegel, there is such a genuinely spiritual *Ineinanderleben,*[30] and this unity of the distinct also characterizes the unity of the family in an ethical as well as anthropological sense.[31] Indeed the 'we self-consciousness,'[32] which for Hegel lies at the basis of all free community, is seen by him as an *Ineinanderleben* of independent self-consciousness in 'mutual recognition.' This *Ineinander-leben* is not an 'immediate' one, however, like that of the hypnotist-patient relation, but a relation of equals mediated precisely by the overcoming of the master-slave relation.[33]

Hegel's concept of a mediated *Ineinanderleben* of independent self-consciousnesses makes possible a notion of polity as a substantial life that is neither: a) an aggregate of atomic egos; nor b) an instinctive or merely natural community. To attain to an ethical relation to another individual where each shares 'equally in ruling and being ruled,' the self, according to Hegel, must have attained to the level of the objective rational consciousness. This means, as the development of the soul has shown, that the individual must be at once both master and slave in his relation to himself as well as his relation to the other. Even to perceive the world as an objective order, I must master myself sufficiently so as to hold myself open to the world as an 'other' or negative of my particular subjectivity. The very attitude of attention requires a strenuousness and a mastery united with an openness and a passivity.[34] In measuring, for example, I am at once active in pursuing my subjective interest and passive in disinterestedly accepting the quantitative results.[35] The *Ineinanderleben* of social living in general, according to Hegel, entailing as it does a thinking in 'names,' makes possible the advance of subjective intelligence beyond sensuous imagery to pure conceptual thinking.[36]

Thus we have seen in what sense, according to Hegel, hypnosis is a regression from the objective consciousness to a psychological master-slave relation. Scientifically the trance is to be understood in terms of the pathway that each self-consciousness takes: from soul to ego, from monadic to objective subjectivity. As implicitly spirit, the passive psychical subjectivity moves to permeate its substantiality by its infusing inner genius. Attaining a mastery of its feeling-life in habit, the subjectivity is able to 'let go' the determinations of its substantiality to form an external order to which it now relates itself as conscious ego. But this very 'letting go' means also a sunderance of the subjectivity from its natural feeling-life, so that the finite ego contains a schism deriving from its very birth. It is this schism—the price of the advance to objectivity—that makes possible a regression to the preobjective level where there can take place the permeation of the feeling-life of one subjectivity by the infusing genius of another. The attainment of independent, objective self-consciousness means that the individual subjectivity has in greater or lesser measure healed the sunderance and united within itself the roles of master and slave. Such a uniting, according to Hegel, is a necessary condition of all forms of *Ineinanderleben* in the realm of ethical life. At the same time, where there is a regression by the finite subjectivity, as in certain morbid states, the *Ineinanderleben* means a relapse from the ethical to the master-slave relation.

It is in this fashion, in terms of a concept of spiritual development on ascending levels of ideality, that Hegel claims at once to explain scientifically the phenomenon of the hypnotic trance and to pass judgment on it as a form of relationship incompatible with that of free spiritual beings.

Notes and References

1. Hegel deals with hypnosis mainly in his *Anthropology*, which forms the first part of his *Philosophy of Mind*. (See below, footnote 2). He usually refers to the phenomenon as 'animal magnetism' or 'magnetic somnambulism', which were the current expressions of his time. The term 'hypnosis' came into use in the 1840's as a result of the work of the English physician James Braid.
2. *Hegel's Philosophy of Mind* (hereafter referred to as HPhM) tr. William Wallace (Oxford 1894), p. 162. Wallace's translation presents the third part of Hegel's *Enzyklopädie der philosophischen Wissenschaften im Grundrisse*, 3rd ed., 1830. (The quoted passage is my own translation.) Wallace's translation does not contain the lecture notes printed in certain German editions, which provide important material for our present study.
3. HPhM p. 197.
4. *Hegel's Science of Logic*, tr. A. V. Miller (London 1969), p. 841.
5. *The Logic of Hegel*, tr. William Wallace (Oxford 1892), p. 207.
6. HPhM p. 196.
7. *The Logic of Hegel*, op. cit., p. 338.
8. *Werke X*, ed. H. Glockner (*Jubiläumsausgabe*, Stuttgart 1958), p. 21.
9. HPhM p. 198 ff.
10. HPhM p. 181.
11. HPhM p. 196.
12. HPhM pp. 179 ff.
13. HPhM pp. 179, 215.
14. *Werke X*, op. cit., p. 217.
15. HPhM p. 181.
16. HPhM p. 186. Hegel adds: 'But it is impossible to say precisely which sensations and which visions he [the patient], in this nominal perception, receives, beholds, and brings to knowledge from his own inward self, and which from the suggestions of the person with whom he stands in relation.' (HPhM p. 187).
17. Hegel, *The Phenomenology of Mind*, tr. J. B. Baillie (London 1931), p. 80.
18. *Werke X*, op. cit., p. 164.
19. HPhM pp. 179, 182.
20. *Werke X*, op. cit., p. 165.
21. HPhM p. 181; *Werke X*, op. cit., p. 165.
22. HPhM p. 184.
23. HPhM pp. 185 ff.
24. HPhM p. 187.
25. *Ibid.*
26. Describing the relationship between Charlie Manson and his 'family,' defendants in the so-called Tate murders, a writer used the expression: 'they became empty vessels for whatever he poured in.' Roberts, Steven V., 'Charlie Manson: One man's family,' *The New York Times Magazine*, Jan. 4, 1970, p. 31.
27. HPhM p. 186.
28. *Nicomachean Ethics* 1134^{b}15.
29. *Cf.* HPhM p. 181.

30. *Hegel's Philosophy of Right*, tr. T. M. Knox (Oxford 1949), pp. 261–62.
31. *Ibid.*, p. 110: HPhM p. 182.
32. *Phenomenology of Mind, op. cit.*, p. 227.
33. Each self-consciousness 'is the mediating term to the other, through which each mediates and unites itself with itself; and each is to itself and to the other an immediate self-existing reality, which, at the same time, exists thus for itself only through this mediation. They recognize themselves as mutually recognizing one another.' (*Ibid.* p. 231).
34. *Werke X, op. cit.*, p. 319.
35. Cf. Royce, Josiah, *The World and the Individual*, 2 vols. (Dover, New York 1959), vol. 1, p. 50.
36. HPhM p. 227.

On Free Agents and Causality:
An Analysis of F_o: P Was Active
In Making A Decision D_1

HERMAN TENNESSEN

University of Alberta

In the present paper I shall endeavor to relate a typical view of one so-called 'libertarian.' I am not primarily concerned with pointing out confusions, let alone 'disproving' the view, but with an attempt at understanding how a libertarian arrives at his position. My contention is that a libertarian is to be understood as a person who is dissatisfied with our empirical conditions and therefore introduces certain *trans-empirical* concepts which lead him to his libertarian and so called 'indeterministic' view. My primary concern in this connexion is the transempirical entities; the 'indeterministic' position and the fatuous notion of 'uncaused decisions' are secondary, something a libertarian only defends because it would otherwise be even more difficult to believe what he apparently insists in believing. There are many types of libertarian views; I shall here confine myself to one example, the view defended by L. J. Russell in his article 'Ought implies can.'[1] I select this article because it is authoritative, and considered in many respects representative of the libertarian view, and because it seems to support my general contention at least in so far as L. J. Russell is to be classified (which I assume): a libertarian.

Russell is in his article first concerned with the relationship between 'causation' and what he calls: '*agency.*' His two main theses may be formulated thus: (a) universal causation, both in its analytic and non-analytic form, is incompatible with 'agency,' and (b) there is an acceptable alternative to the doctrine of universal causation—involving the possibility of what Russell calls: 'changing and indefinite properties

E

with definite upper and lower limits'—and 'agency' *is* compatible with *this* view.

Russell argues that the thesis of what he calls 'universal *non*-analytic causation' is 'completely unverifiable and useless' (p. 163). I shall choose not to discuss this claim here.

The doctrine of 'universal analytic causation' is formulated by Russell in the following way: 'every determinate characteristic of every state of every thing in the universe is capable of being connected by some causal law, or some combination of causal laws, with some determinate characteristics of states, and shown to be relatively independent of others.' (p. 160). He offers no explanation as to how 'agency' may be compatible with 'causation,' in this sense of 'causation.' He neither defines nor precises what he intends to mean by his term 'agency,' all he does is to describe certain states of affairs which, according to his view, exclude agency. He says ' . . . in so far as there is a causal law which involves that A in state a_1 partially characterized by p_1 under conditions c_1 at the time t_1 will be in state a_2 partially characterized by p_2 at time t_2, it does not seem possible to speak of A as active in respect of this change from p_1 to p_2' (p. 164). And he goes on: 'in so far as a feeling of making effort, in conjunction with the thought of a particular end to be attained, plays an important part as a causal factor in the events which will next occur . . . we speak of the individual as being active . . . But if every one of the factors arising in him is itself completely determined by a complex of causal factors . . . *we can only say* that the choice *occurs* and not . . . that the individual *chooses*' (p. 166— my *italics*). These suggestions are not terribly helpful. The important question seems to be: *in what sense* (or in what senses) *of the expressions 'P was active' or 'P chose' is it false to assert that P chose the action A_1 or was active in bringing about the decision D_1* if we assume that D_1 and A_1 were caused? Russell really says very little about this. The reader must try to construct interpretations. We shall here start with some suggestions for interpretations of *'P was active in making D_1'* (F_0) which do not, at the face of it, seem to conflict with Russell's doctrine of universal analytic causation, and then try to ascertain whether at least one plausible interpretation may be found which is not inconsistent with this doctrine.

Let us say that Russell by F_0, intends to signify that P_1 *before making D_1, thought about the consequences and characteristics of A_1 and about the alternative(s) to A^1 (A^2), considered which norms (values) would be affected by A_1 and A_2, tried to find out which of them would best realize his norms and values, finally concluding that A_1 would be* *that action.* Let us refer to this as P's *'activity,'$_1$* and the whole sentence as 'F_1.' It is, I think, beyond doubt that quite often when we utter F_0, we may intend to convey this something in the direction of F_1 or something cognitively very close to it. But F_0, interpreted in this way (i.e., the interpretation, F_1), does not contradict plausible interpretations of Russell's doctrine of universal analytic causation. Russell may very well agree to this, but maintains that the interpretation is unacceptable. The above quotation seems to indicate one reason why Russell might *not* be satisfied with F_1: F_1 does not imply that P's *activity^1 was a casual factor bringing about D^1.* But even if we change F_1 in such a way that this *is* asserted (let us call this new interpretation F_2), Russell, I think, would find F_2 just as irrelevant as F_1, because F_2 (just as does F_1) does not exclude the possibility that P's activity$_1$ *'just occurred'* and that P was not *active in bringing it about.* Let us therefore change F_2 so as to better meet with this requirement. Suppose that by F_0 we mean to say that *P, before starting to consider whether he should make D_1 or not, thought about different types of decision-making, studying their different advantages and disadvantages, concluding that considering the consequences of A_1 and A_2 with reference to the norms and values affected, would be the best policy, given certain norms or values,* (let us refer to this activity as 'activity'$_2$), *let us furthermore suppose that F_3 also asserts that activity$_2$ was a causal factor in bringing about activity$_1$, and that F_2 also is entailed.* Let us call this compound interpretation: F_3. I do not think that, by F_0, we often intend to convey anything in the direction of what F_3 may reasonably be assumed to assert. Nevertheless, it *may* be what Russell would have chosen to mean by F_0, had he ever thought of it. However: F_3 is not likely to be interpreted as inconsistent with the contention that D_1 is caused.

Ultimately Russell would probably find F_3 rather unsatisfactory for very much the same reason as he would F_2. For F_3 does not seem to exclude the possibility that p's activity$_2$ *'just occurred,'* without P being *active* in bringing it about. And there are apparently no obvious reasons why we should feel compelled to try to modify F_3 in the way in which we modified F_2, because the question: 'Was P active in bringing about his activity$_x$?' may *always* be asked under any circumstances. Hence I shall argue that the maxim not to call an activity 'an activity' unless it is the result of a previous activity, leads to a *regressus ad infinitum, ad nauseum usque.* But Russell does not say that we are bound to postulate an infinite series of activities in order to say that a person decided. Psychologically speaking, such a series seems nonsensical.

Moreover: when saying that P was active or when distinguishing between a person as being active or inactive, our criterion, I suppose is
surely not to be understood in terms of a question as to whether or not
this nonsenical series has taken place. Finally, if Russell did postulate
this nonsense, F^3 would still not conflict with his doctrine of causation.
On the other hand, Russell *could* be interpreted to have intended to
say that in order to avoid this infinite regress, we should assume that
one of the activities in this series—say, activity$_2$—is not causally connected to any other factors in the universe, and that this assumption
conflicts with his doctrine of causation. I think we are bound to accept
that such a conflict may be formulated. But would it not rather seem
like a conflict between saying 'everything is caused' and 'something
is not caused'? It would certainly not be a conflict between *'causation'*
and *'agency'*!

Let us, however, before proceeding further, raise the following question: Is it plausible to assume that Russell intends to say that there is
something fishy or peculiar about P's *action* or *decision* or *activity$_1$,*
and that this makes it reasonable or acceptable to say that P was active
in bringing them about (in spite of the fact that they were actually
caused)? Whereas we cannot say that P was active in bringing about
activity$_2$ or activity$_3$ etc., if they were caused? It does not, at the face of
it, seem plausible to assume this, for Russell says: 'It seems clear that
on the view I am following out it is necessary to accept the conclusion
that an act^2 is an 'uncaused cause' (p. 182). Hence, it seems that we can
forget about all sorts of series of activities, for he seems to want to say
that in his sense of 'being active,' it is false to say that P was active in
bringing about D$_1$ even if D$_1$ was in fact caused by P's activity$_1$, and
activity$_1$ by activity$_2$, and so forth. Hence his position (as indicated
ibid. p. 166), quoted earlier, does not seem compatible with his inten-
tion as conveyed above. That D$_1$ was caused by activity$_1$ is neither
necessary nor sufficient for asserting that P chose D$_1$; on the contrary,
if D$_1$ was *caused* by activity$_1$, then P was *not* active in bringing about
D$_1$. Very confusing, indeed!

Let us try a different line. Russell may have been reasoning in
(roughly) the following way: If we can derive from a certain 'law of
nature' that P, in the situation of S with 100 per cent probability (or:
certainty) would decide D$_1$, then P could not (if we assume the conditions to be unchanged) have decided D$_2$. This position, however, cannot be acceptable to Russell because he does not seem to be concerned
with the question whether *P could have decided otherwise,* only with
the question whether we *'can say'*: *'P was active in bringing about*

D_1.' Perhaps his position is that if P could not decide otherwise, then P did not choose D_1, since no other decision was available. This, of course, is correct if and only if it merely means that since it was 100 per cent probable that D_1 would be the choice, the probability was zero that, say, D_2 would be chosen. But it does not follow that 'no other decision was *possible*' in any other sense than just this. Another decision, D_2, *was possible, e.g.* in the sense that the hypothetico-deductive system from which the prediction was derived, may turn out to be untenable, disproved, etc. or in the sense that it is *not self-contradictory,* or it does not entail a logical contradiction to assert that D_2 might have been the choice of P in S.

Russell, I suppose, might want to answer that none of these senses of 'D_2 was possible' is really relevant, since the crucial question is whether P, in S, had it *in his power,* to make another decision. In order to say that P, in S, made D_1, we must claim that P, in S, had it in his power to decide otherwise; and—so Russell might argue—if D_1 was caused, then P did not have such power. If we take the expression 'to have D_2 in one's power' in an empirical sense, as when we say that P has it in his power to read, or to walk, or to speak, etc., then our power to bring about something is in no way delimited by postulating principles of causality. Our power to do something, e.g. to make a decision, may be limited by many different factors, but it is never a principle of causality that blocks or limits our power.[3] If our decisions were caused up till this day, but would be uncaused from 8 o'clock tonight, there is no reason whatsoever to expect that from that moment on we would have more *power* than before, to overcome, say, (morally) bad inclinations. And the difference between asserting 'P has power to make D_2' and 'P had power to make D_2' is not in any way subtler than the difference between 'P *is* aggressive' and 'P *was* aggressive.' But Russell, I take it, will object that power in this empirical sense of 'power,' is quite insufficient to ensure that P in all situations, not only in 'indifference-situations,' can overcome any degree of inner resistance (*vide* p. 184). Hence, we seem to be forced to assume that Russell will imply that we, as human beings, possess some sort of '*trans*empirical power centre,' as it were. If this is his point it also becomes understandable how he can permit himself to arrive at the conclusion that 'P chose D_1' is inconsistent with his doctrine of causality: Suppose that, when Russell asserts that P chose D_1, he implies that P had it in his power to choose D_2 in the sense that he had a trans-empirical power centre strong enough to overcome all resistance against making D_2. A behaviorist oriented scientist might then object as follows: I don't know

E*

whether any of P's decisions are, or could be, influenced by any such a power centre. I don't even understand what could plausibly be meant by this expression. But I do not see why I should have to worry about it at all. I can predict every characteristic of P's decision without paying any attention to the operation of mythical 'transempirical power centres.' If a libertarian wants to safeguard his belief by postulating the existence of such a power centre, he probably will want to refute this objection. This he may try to do by maintaining that 'exact predictions are impossible,' because the power centre manifests itself in a way which, for the scientist, may appear as more or less random.

According to this interpretation, then F_0 asserts that P, in S, had it in his power to decide D_2 instead of D_1 in the sense that *P has a transempirical power centre which is strong enough to overcome any degree of inner resistance and which, within certain limits, manifests itself irregularly* (F_4). Although F_4 seems to fit in with some of Russell's possible positions, it does not cover all that he intends to convey by his concept of 'agency.' For it is rather odd, maybe even unbelievable, that Russell should maintain that P was active in S if and only if F_4 were true. F_4 may be true although P, in S, was completely unconscious. F_4 tells us nothing about what happened *to* or *in* P (in S), whereas F_0 makes it explicit that P was *active*. Hence, in order to render Russell's view somewhat less implausible, we shall have to attempt to combine F_4 with F_1. F_0 is thus interpreted to assert that *P's decision D_1 in S, was preceded by activity$_1$ (but not caused by it), and that P had it in his power to decide otherwise in the sense indicated* (F_5).

According to Russell, activity$_1$, should not be considered a cause of D_1. He seems to hold that activity presents the agent with *reasons* for or against D_1 and D_2; and: 'reasons are not causes' (p. 184). The concept, 'reason' certainly seems, at the face of it, different from the concept, 'cause,' but causes and reasons may be closely related. My reason for deciding not to walk street X may be that it is dirty. The *cause* of my decision not to walk street X may be my expectation that I shall find it dirty, plus my desire to avoid getting dirt on my shoes. To say that our decisions have reasons do not, of course, imply that they are uncaused. But Russell does not only assert that we decide on the basis of reasons (I interpret his term 'grounds' as cognitively similar to 'reasons'), but that our decisions are *uncaused*! Hence, the question arises: Does Russell want to claim that activity in the sense of 'activity$_1$' is completely superfluous? Does he hold that whether P shall make a decision D_1, or D_2, is entirely independent of this activity? This view is indeed so strange, that it would appear uncharitable to interpret

Russell to maintain such a position. Hence we must assume that he is seeing *some kind* of connexion between activity$_1$ and P's decision D$_1$, although he does seem to want to exclude the possibility of any causal connexions.

Russell seems to conceive of this connexion in analogy with a judge's relationship to his documents. The judge reads one document after another, but they do not *cause* a finite verdict. The judge *makes the decision*. This is fine as far as it goes. But how are we to describe the relationship between a) the impulses experienced by the judge while reading the documents and b) his decision? Are these impulses also some kind of documents read by the judge, or may they not influence him in a rather causal sort of way? If we take the former view, what then about the (meta-) impulses experienced on this second-order reading of the documents? Are they also 'just considered' by the judge, or do they causally influence him? etc., *ad infinitum*. If one sticks to this judge–documented–model, it becomes rather inexplicable that a decision ever is being made, or one must conceive of the decision as in one sense or other *being made by the judge without being causally influenced by the factors,* the reading of (the reading of . . .) documents.

An example may shed some light on this dilemma: Smith has decided to marry Simone, and we make the assertion 'John Smith's decision to marry Simone is *not* causally related to any other factors in the universe, but it was nevertheless made by John Smith.' Is there any plausible interpretation of this statement? Suppose Smith objects: 'My decision to marry Simone was made by me, because it was caused by my passionate love for her.' Russell, then, would have to answer that Smith did not make that decision since it was caused by Smith's passions. And no matter which factors Mr. Smith mentions: his hopes, his expectations, his heterosexuality, his values, his loneliness, etc., Russell would always have to answer that a decision caused by such or similar or possibly any factors, was *not* made by Mr. Smith. Challenged by Smith as to the nature of Smith's self or ego, Russell might answer e.g. that a person's ego is a pure ego, the scene where activity takes place, or that it is a centre of activity, but of an activity of transempirical nature or origin.

If Russell's notion of 'the ego' should correspond with either of these alternatives, it again becomes understandable why he permits himself to maintain that 'agency' is incompatible with his doctrine of causation. If he maintains that our ego is transempirical, he may defend, for the reasons mentioned in connexion with the transempirical power centre, that our decisions are uncaused. If he accepts the other view, however he may come to the same position by adopting the following argumentational preferences: 'a decision must not be *causally* related to any non-pure ego factors in order to be made by the agent.' A person's pure ego by definition—cannot function as a cause factor. Hence, if P's decision shall be said to be made by P, it must be uncaused, *viz.* made by P's pure ego.

Of these two interpretations it seems most friendly to select the transempirical one, because it simplifies matters. We may already have interpreted Russell to maintain that we all have something, which may (not too misleadingly) be called: 'a transempirical power centre.' If we now assume that this alleged power centre is part of a 'transempirical ego,' then a certain intimacy is obtained between the ego and the power centre. If we choose not to select this interpretation, the following objection may be made: That P has a transempirical power centre shows only *that there is power in P, not that P has power. What guarantees that P has it in his power to operate his transempirical power centre?* On the above grounds, this question seems to become rather meaningless, as the power centre was assumed to be part of that transempirical whole which constitutes the ego.

Now, what (if indeed anything) is a libertarian of this type to make of the relationship between activity$_1$, the decision D$_1$ and P's transempirical ego? In order to say that P was active in bringing about D$_1$, he will probably be inclined to require that activity$_1$ was what he might call an 'activity of P's transempirical ego.' Otherwise, the activity should have to be said to *'just occur'* without carrying the mark of his ego. This activity, on the other hand, is not to be seen as a cause of his decision, because the decision is by definition not caused at all. The constellation of forces preceding the decision is a unique constellation, just as the constellation of forces preceding a historical event. And if we talk about D$_1$ as being caused only if we can assume repetitions, we cannot talk about D$_1$ as being caused. Russell, it seems, may therefore well be suspected to think that activity$_1$ is a necessary condition for, but not a cause of , the decision.

We may now construct an interpretation of F$_0$ ('P, in S, was active in making D$_1$'), which seems fairly consistent with Russell's view, when carefully considering his article *in toto*.

F$_0$ may apparently be interpreted in a direction stated roughly as follows: (i) P, in S, thought about the consequences and characteristics of A$_1$ and A$_2$, and tried to find out which of them would best realize P's norms (or values); concluding that A$_1$ would be that action, and (ii) this activity was an activity of P's transempirical ego, and (iii) it was also a necessary condition for (but not a cause of) D_1 being the result of the decision process, and (iv) P, in S, had it in his power to decide D_2 instead of D_1, in the sense that P's transempirical ego includes a transempirical power centre which is strong enough to make D_2, no matter what D_2 is, and (v) this transempirical ego manifests itself, within certain limits, in irregular ways (F_6).

I do not know whether Russell would be wise enough to accept this interpretation; most probably he would not. For my own part I find it very hard to comprehend what F_6 asserts, but I think I understand it to some degree, and that I realize how one may possibly arrive at a view like this. The crucial factor seems to be the degree to which one is (dis)satisfied with ones empirical conditions. If one accepts that man's power to decide is limited, and that it varies from person to person and from situation to situation, as it does if one takes 'power' in an empirical sense, then there is no reason why one should want to assume or believe in transempirical power centres. On the other hand, if this empirical notion of 'power' is felt as an insult to man's self-image, or as undermining man's right to assume that he always had it in his power to decide otherwise, then one may inflate man's empirical power until one cannot get room for it in an individual person, one has to make it 'spiritual,' 'transempirical,' or something of that order.

If F_6 is accepted as a plausible interpretation, we may be in the position to explain why Russell maintains not only that P's decision is uncaused, but that it is uncaused only within certain limits. Russell introduces the concept of a property which is indefinite within certain limits. He seems to believe that a decision in some way 'arises in connexion with' (p. 182) a property of this kind, but he does not offer any further clarification. What he intends to say is possibly this: suppose we could study P's decision-making in n instances of the same situation S where P every time should choose between the alternatives A_1, A_2, A_3 and A_4, and where he every time had the same perceptions, cognitions, desires, etc. Suppose, furthermore, that we could give scientifically based predictions to the effect, that he would not choose A_1 and A_4 but no matter how much knowledge we got (at least at our present stage of insight) the choice between A_2 and A_3 would be, as we might choose to put it: 'indefinite.' The result of the decision process would then be indefinite within certain limits. Let us return to John Smith: Mr. Smith is this time trying to make up his mind whether to marry Miss A, Miss B, Miss C or Miss D (the four of them being his only possible candidates for marriage). If we could predict that Mr. Smith would definitely not decide in favour of Miss A or Miss

D, but were (presently, at least) unable to predict—even after an enormous increase in our knowledge—whether he would select Miss B or Miss C, then—if Smith decides, say, for Miss B—his decision would probably be an example of what Russell means by 'a decision, uncaused within certain limits.' His final decision (D_1) in favour of Miss B would 'provide a definite outcome within these limits' (p. 182). It is important to make it clear, however, that *even if we were faced with a situation of this kind, there would be no reason why we should conclude that the choice of D_1 was due to P's activity; and there would be no reason why we should say that D_1 was due to P's activity rather than saying that his predictable refusal of Miss A was due to his activity. We should only be entitled to say that the one outcome was predictable, the other (Miss B or Miss C) unpredictable.* In order to be able to conclude, as Russell wants to do, that D_1 was the result of P's activity, we have to know something else, *viz.* that D_1 was brought about through P's activity. As we have seen, Russell is rather reluctant to accept this if D_1 appears to be caused by activity$_1$. He might, however, agree to say so *if D_1 was the result of an activity of P's transempirical ego.* But from the assumption that D_1 is unpredictable it does not follow that D_1 is the result of an activity of this or of any other special kind. Why, then, does Russell postulate that decisions are causally indefinite within certain limits? A plausible conjecture here is that he perceives predictability as a threat to his right to assume or believe in a transempirical activity. If the outcome of a decision process is indefinite within certain limits, so Russell seems to want to argue, then the predicting scientist cannot shave away the concepts of 'a transempirical power centre' and 'a transempirical ego' by any Occam's razor. One is free to believe that the uncertainty is due to the fact that this transempirical entity manifests itself in a way which to the scientist may appear as partly random. If the belief in indeterminacy is a safeguard of this kind, then even a small degree of indeterminacy may do. Hence, it is apparent why Russell would declare himself satisfied with the belief that our decisions are causally indefinite within certain limits. Intersubjective evidence cannot in any given instance corroborate the hypothesis that a person was active in sense F_6, because such evidence as regards (ii), (iii), (iv) and (v) is not available. (*vide* p. 11). We may, however, possibly acquire reasons to support the claim that decisions are *not* the result of an F_6 activity. We may find, say, that (i) is not fulfilled; and from the fact that we can give a causal explanation of a decision, we can now infer that there is no uncertainty zone, and that consequently (v) is not fulfilled. In other words: P was (in S) *not* active in sense F_6. It is, more generally, exceedingly difficult to see what on earth should compel us to believe that when we consider an agent responsible, his behavior should necessarily be the result of an F_6-activity; we do in any event hold people responsible for their negligences and omissions. And, on the other hand, even if the agent's behavior were an end product of F_6-activity, he is *not* responsible provided he was, or believed he was powerless to decide otherwise, and did not have it *in his power* to believe anything else.

Needless to say, the above tentative and superficial reflections, exposing one libertarian's futile attempts to make sense of his position (including, in some cases, 'indeterminism,' 'uncaused decisions' or 'uncaused acts,' *etc.*), should not tempt one to look to the opposite position ('determinism,' 'fatalism' and what not) for a more tenable point of departure. Unfortunately, the opposite to (or the negation or contradiction of) nonsense, is not sense, but just *another* kind of nonsense.

Notes and References

1. *Proceedings of the Aristotelian Society*, Vol. 36.
2. Russell does not, in this connexion, make any detectable attempt to distinguish 'action' and 'decision.' *Vide*, p. 180.
3. *Vide*: H. Ofstad: *An Inquiry into the Freedom of Decision*, (Ch. VI, Oslo, London, 1961). The notion of 'inner resistance' is just in the following as introduced by Ofstad, *ibid*.

Persons: Private and Public

KENNETH E. HAAS

Hamline University

The aim of this paper is to explore the inherent duality between 'private' and 'public' in the notion of person and to argue that 'person' is a term of moral and social significance only. In other words, persons do not have any ontological status independently of a moral and social domain. The distinction between the 'private' and 'public' aspects of personal existence originates in the difference between identifying responsible agents and describing and assessing certain relations among responsible agents. The distinction is not to be understood as the result of distinguishing between oneself as a self-conscious being and other things in the world. The concept of person is not, then, part of the subject-matter of philosophical psychology but of ethical and social philosophy. I will try to make this case by examining the general thesis of the con- tractual nature of society and Locke's theory of personal identity. Finally, I will state my positive view.

1. Social contract theories, in which the concept of person seems first to have appeared in modern philosophy,[1] are essentially ambiguous concerning the nature and existence of persons. Social contract theorists may be expected to agree with Hobbes that 'concord amongst men is artificial, and by way of covenant.'[2] But there is no consensus about the nature of the individuals who make the social covenant or their status once the contract is made. Of course, social contract theorists agree that the individuals who enter into the contract are men and that the individuals who remain after the contract takes force are men. Yet the contract's implications are so profound that it is necessary to distin- guish in some way the former individuals from the latter individuals. The latter men are, so to speak, men by art or convention, and the former men are men by nature. The difference between men-in-society

and men-in-nature, or between those who live according to 'civil law' and those who live according to 'natural law,' is crucial enough to warrant reference to those who live according to civil law as 'persons.'

While there is sufficient reason for using the term 'person' to refer to beings who live according to civil law, social contract theorists do not consistently use the term in this fashion. Although you may detect a shift in Rousseau's discussions about *men* in the state of nature and *person* in the state of society, the shift is less apparent in Hobbes and hardly to be found in Locke at all.[3] However, if we direct our attention to the implications of the notion of a social contract, it is clear that natural man cannot be a political animal and cannot be said to have a 'public' or 'civil' life. A natural man, whether he lives a life of war against every other man or a life of freedom and peace, cannot live according to anything we might call a code of laws, or an explicit set of rights and duties. Rousseau states this fundamental principle very simply, '. . . the social order is a sacred right which serves for the basis of all others. Yet this right comes not from nature; it is therefore founded on conventions.'[4] A natural man does not, as does a social man or a person, live a life of obligations, duties, rights, and privileges.

The fundamental difference between 'natural man' and 'social man' leads to a dilemma for social contract theory, and this dilemma points to the origin of most objections to the theory. The problem is, How is it possible for a social contract to be made unless there are responsible individuals to make it? If it is because of the contract that rights and duties come to be, that there are such things as 'responsible individuals,' then it is not true, after all, that responsible individuals and their rights and duties come to be within a society. For the making of a contract *presupposes* the existence of responsible individuals. This means, presumably, that natural man *does* have obligations, duties, rights, and privileges. If, however, this is true, then it is false that the social contract is a right which serves as the basis of all others. This problem suggests that the origin of the difficulties in social contract theories is not so much the notion of the contract as it is the existential and moral nature of the individuals who make the contract. Social contract theorists raise the problem of the nature of persons because their view results in ambiguities about the individuals who make the social contract. Their view trades on the duality of 'private' and 'public' in the concept of person.

2. Locke's discussion of personal identity is especially instructive for the way in which it brings to light this duality. Locke's approach to

the nature of personal identity is expressly metaphysical. The metaphysical issue is, roughly speaking, the problem of individuality, and in seeking a solution for this problem, Locke proposes various criteria of identity. He begins with an observation about identity in general.

> For we never finding nor conceiving it possible that two things of the same kind should exist in the same place at the same time, we rightly conclude that whatever exists anywhere at any time, excludes all of the same kind, and is there itself alone. When therefore we demand whether anything be the same or no, it refers always to something that existed such a time in such a place, which it was certain, at that instant, was the same with itself, and no other; . . .[5]

Locke's analysis then spells out the implications of this statement. First, he states the principle in terms of which it is impossible for two things of the same kind (whatever the kind) to exist in the same place at the same time. This is the so-called principle of individuation which, according to Locke, is 'existence itself.' In virtue of the simple fact of existence, the individuality of anything that exists is guaranteed. This principle, however, does not make explicit the conditions of identity upon which we base our judgment that an entity of a certain kind is 'the same.' In other words, the principle of individuation does not say specifically what prevents various entities of the same kind from being in the same place at the same time. In order to state specific criteria of identity, it is necessary to reflect on the various types of entities with a view to discovering what makes an individual of a particular kind *one* individual. Second, Locke moves from the general problem of what makes anything at all an individual to what makes a 'piece of matter,' say, an atom, an individual, and from this to the 'identity of vegetables,' the 'identity of brutes,' the 'identity of men,' and finally the 'identity of persons.' The problem of individuality, in short, is carried to increasingly narrower classes of entities and successively different criteria of identity are developed.

From the outset, it is evident that Locke takes persons to be a kind of entity in a system of different kinds of entities. The criterion for the individuality of any person is not the same as the criterion for the individuality of a man, or animal, or plant, or piece of matter. What guarantees the individuality of a person, according to Locke, is 'consciousness.' Consciousness is what makes it impossible for two persons to exist in the same place at the same time. In consciousness, the individuality and incommunicability, that is, the privacy, of a person is founded. And, although 'in our ordinary way of speaking,' Locke says, 'the same person and the same man stand for one and the same thing,' this is due to insufficient attention to the ideas for which 'person' and 'man' stand, By 'person,' we really have in mind any consciousness, human or otherwise; by 'man,' we have in mind an animal of a particular form.

But this is not all there is to Locke's account, for to be a person is not merely to be an entity that possesses consciousness. He adds, 'in this *personal identity* is founded all the right and justice of reward and punishment; happiness and misery being that for which every one is concerned for *himself,* not mattering what becomes of any substance not joined to or affected with that consciousness.'[6] And later, almost at the close of his account, he observes that person '. . . is a forensic term appropriating actions and their merit; and so belongs only to intelligent agents capable of a law, and happiness and misery.'[7] Here Locke introduces another, and a fundamentally different, aspect of the notion of person. His initial aim was ontological in character, namely, to say what kind of being is denoted by the word 'person.' But within the pursuit of the ontological question, Locke finds it necessary to include moral or social aspects of personal existence.

Contractual theories of society have in common the thesis that rights and duties come to be only within a social order. If 'person' is a forensic term that applies only to intelligent agents capable of a law and having to do with the moral assessment of actions, then persons are and must be social beings. By hypothesis, persons cannot exist by nature. If persons existed by nature, then rights and duties would exist by nature; and, if rights and duties exist by nature, the thesis that rights and duties come to be only within a social order must be rejected. On the other hand, if 'person' is an ontological term, it denotes a particular kind of natural entity. It has to do with the individuality and incommunicability of conscious beings, that is, it refers to that which makes it impossible for two persons to exist in the same place at the same time. By hypothesis, persons cannot exist by convention. To say that persons exist by convention is to say that consciousness exists by convention, and this is clearly a peculiar view. One of the consequences of this view would be that the individuality of a person is a matter of convention, and I can think of no one who has been prepared to assert this. If, then, persons do not exist by convention but by nature, we are forced to reject the thesis that society is a result of convention. This could be avoided, I imagine, by asserting the existence of two kinds of persons in the universe, but such a distinction would merely postpone the difficulty.

Although Locke tried to show the connection between the metaphysical person and the social and moral person, his appraisal of the connection seems to be unsatisfactory. He says that in virtue of being a metaphysical person, an entity becomes by that same fact a social and moral person. This may be true, but it entails saying that society and the rights and duties that come to be within society are as natural as personal existence is—all of which contradicts the social contract theory.

The structure of Locke's theory of personal identity has influenced subsequent theories concerning the nature of persons.[8] For philosophers following Locke have taken the concept of person as having an ontological reference which must be understood if its moral and social import is to be understood. Since this procedure trades on and exemplifies the duality of 'private' and 'public' in the notion of person, it leads to identifying the question of the nature of personal existence with knotty problems about the knowledge of other minds, the relation of mind and body, and it leads to artificial and *ad hoc* theories of the relation between individuals and society. In the remainder of this paper, I would like to suggest how the concept of person is related particularly to the last of these issues and how 'person' is a term that has bearing only on the ethical and social issue.

3. So far, I have tried to indicate how social contract theories lead to difficulties by treating the concept of person ambiguously, and how Locke's theory of personal identity manifests this ambiguity. Against this general view, I want to argue that 'person' has social and moral significance alone and that its ontological significance consists in its application within a social and moral domain. Accordingly, the content of the concept of person is to be explicated in terms of 'character' and 'responsibility.' A person is a character-exhibiting, responsible individual.

The asumption that persons are a kind of entity, *i.e.* that 'person' stands for something, is a precarious assumption—not, however, because it is ontological in character, nor because it implies that 'person' denotes a kind of entity. What is misleading is the assumption's implication that we have access to the ontological reference of 'person' independently of its social and moral reference. This is objectionable for two reasons. One is that we are led to believe that the nature of personal existence is ascertainable independently of an inquiry into the social and moral aspect of personal existence, and this is an open question. The other is that we are led to infer that the social and moral aspect of personal existence is to be understood, or analyzed, in terms of the ontological status of persons. In other words, the supposition that the notion of person has ontological implications as *opposed to* social and moral implications virtually commits one to saying that all features of social and moral life are consequences of the ontological character of personal existence.

It is tempting to say, as Locke and others have done, that the implicit reference to 'privacy,' or 'individuality,' in the concept of person must be connected with self-identification and, therefore, with self-consciousness. For ordinary life is replete with occasions for keeping straight what belongs to oneself and what does not so belong. Men guard their personal effects jealously, the personal lives of movie stars are subject-matter for lurid speculation, and so on. In these and other references to persons, the subject of observation and discussion is evidently a particular human individual or something that belongs to, or is possessed by, or is characteristic of, a particular human individual. But the bare fact of self-identification is sufficient to explain only a few of such references, and even in these cases, 'person' is a term used primarily of oneself. Given the multiplicity of such references, a difficult epistemic problem arises when we attempt to explain how, on the basis of self-consciousness, it is possible to refer to other persons or 'selves.' Mere awareness of one's own particularity of one's own differences from everything else, does not involve the recognition of other persons or 'selves.' Further, we do not *infer* that other persons exist on the grounds that some entity is self-conscious and, consequently, others of a like kind ought to be self-conscious—even if it were true, which it is not, that self-consciousness is attributable to all entities that are persons.

It may be true that no individual needs evidence of its own existence as a person, but we do need evidence for the existence of others as persons, and we do need procedures for deciding what is and what is not a person. In brief, the *recognition* of one's own particularity is unimportant and uninformative so far as the concept of person is concerned, because the private aspect of personal existence has nothing specifically to do with such recognition. What is relevant to the private aspect of personal existence is 'character.' I choose the term 'character' because it points to the dramatic origin of the concept of person. In Greek and Roman theater, various characters were identified by their masks, their *personae,* and we may turn to this theatrical source for enlightenment about the individuality of personal existence. Because characters are identified by a visible mask, the notion of a person is partly empirical in origin. This suggests that the private aspect of personal existence is connected with the identification of certain individuals, but not necessarily with self-identification. It is not from introspection as such that we derive the notion of a person; rather, it is from our perception of the 'visible mask,' or exhibition of character, of a particular individual.

The character which an individual exhibits is appropriately designated by the word 'personality.' We take an individual's personality as its alone, as the locus of its distinctiveness. It is wrong to internalize personality and to regard it as a mysterious force within the cranium or processes of thought. We identify persons by recognizing the myriad of features each displays, by seeing whatever makes an individual distinguishable from its surroundings. Personalities are publicly available. This does not mean that an individual's personality is completely open and transparent to casual inspection, but it is not necessary to know everything there is to know about an individual in order to be able to identify it. The privacy of personal existence is the exhibition of individual character.

Persons are identified within a system of individuals, some of which are persons, and the public, or forensic, side of personal existence must be understood in terms of the persons in this system. In the forensic sense, a person is a responsible agent, and a person must have the capacity to act, and be responsible for its actions, within this domain. The added requirement that a person must be a responsible agent narrows the application of 'person' within the domain of individuals. An individual may possess a personality, *i.e.* exhibit character, without being a responsible agent, and accordingly having a personality, in the specified sense, is not a sufficient condition for personal existence. But, while some individuals that exhibit character are not responsible agents, it seems clear that all responsible agents, corporate or human, are character-exhibiting individuals. A person is a responsible agent and, therefore, a character-exhibiting individual.

The connection between the 'private' and 'public' aspects of personal existence must be understood, then, in reverse of the way in which social contract theorists take it. No analysis of the concept of person is possible without reference to the notion of a responsible agent, and it is essential to begin with the notion of a responsible agent in order to give an account of the connection between the 'private' and 'public' aspects of personal existence. Given that there are responsible agents, it is necessary to be able to identify them, since the determination of responsibility involves identifying a particular individual in a system of individuals. But the problem of identification is independent of the determination of responsibility, and the development of criteria of identity has bearing on 'personal identity' only when it is given that a person is necessarily a responsible agent.

To put this another way, the 'private' and 'public' sides of personal existence are correlative and coterminous. The problem of identifying persons is not, strictly speaking, connected with the 'private' aspect of the concept of person *until* it is established that persons are responsible agents. When, for example, Locke stated a criterion for 'personal identity,' he was talking merely about the identity of self-conscious beings *until* he made the additional stipulation that all responsible agents are self-conscious beings.[9] The 'public' aspect of the concept of person refers to the domain of action and individuals within which a person is held responsible and identified. From this it follows, as I have tried to show, that persons do not have any ontological status independently of their social and moral status. A person is a social and moral entity, and any inquiry into its ontological status must begin with this fact. A person is not a quasi-physical entity whose properties are discoverable by introspection or any other particular method. The ontological status of persons *is* moral and social.

The account of the relation between the 'private' and 'public' sides of personal existence that I am proposing has one thing in common with social contract theories, namely, the belief that rights and duties, and right and duty bearing entities, exist only in societies. However, where social contract theorists maintain that the social order and the rights and duties within the social order are conventional, it seems, on the contrary, that conventions are intelligible only if it is given that there is a system of responsible and identifiable agents. The existence of a social order does not necessarily presuppose a first convention. Rather, a first convention necessarily presupposes the existence of responsible agents. We have no need of the hypothesis of a social contract, and the problem that the social contract was intended to solve, 'How does one justify the use of force in a society?', will have to be solved along other lines. Men do not have to make themselves or their institutions into responsible agents, even though we are sometimes in the dark about what our responsibilities are, and even though some of our responsibilities are conventional. Nor do men have to make their own character, even though their character is amenable to their control. We are naturally responsible agents and, therefore, social beings.

4. I have tried to show that 'person' is a term which has application only within a social and moral domain, and that persons do not exist

apart from a social and moral domain. If this analysis is essentially correct, then the concept of person is a moral and social notion, not a psychological one. The introduction of the concept of person in the context of problems about solipsism, or the nature of self-consciousness, or knowledge of other minds, is a misuse of the notion. I tried to make these points by showing how social contract theorists have misunderstood the duality of 'private' and 'public' in the concept of person, and how their view results in obscuring the concept of person in its connection with social and moral domains.

Notes and References

1. See Thomas Hobbes, *Leviathan*, Part I, Chapter 16, 'Of Persons, Authors, and Things Personated.'
2. Thomas Hobbes, *De Corpore Politico* in *Body, Man, and Citizen*, Richard S. Peters (ed.). (New York: The Crowell-Collier Publishing Co., 1962). p. 309.
3. See John Locke, *Two Treatises of Civil Government* (London: J. M. Dent & Sons, Ltd., 1962), pp. 159–161.
4. Jean Jacques Rousseau, *The Social Contract*, Charles Frankel (ed.). (New York: Hafner Publishing Co., 1947), p. 6.
5. John Locke, *An Essay Concerning Human Understanding*, John W. Yolton (ed.). (London: J. M. Dent & Sons, Ltd., 1965), I, p. 274.
6. *Ibid.*, p. 287. Locke's italics.
7. *Ibid.*, p. 291.
8. See for example, P. F. Strawson, *Individuals* (Garden City, N.Y.: Doubleday & Co., Inc., 1963), pp. 81–113.
9. It is not entirely clear that Locke did make this stipulation because he seems to have argued that all self-conscious beings are responsible agents, *not* that all responsible agents are self-conscious beings.

The Language of Actions

RUTH MACKLIN

Case Western Reserve University

In contemporary philosophy of action, there is a commonly held view that human actions are properly to be explained by providing reasons for acting rather than causes of action. Although I do not intend to argue here either for or against this claim, I would like to point out an issue which appears to underlie this dispute. This issue concerns some features of the language we employ in reporting and describing actions —features which are crucial for an understanding of and solution to the many problems regarding human actions. An examination of the language of actions is logically prior to the epistemological and ethical inquiries which form the core of current philosophical interest in the topic of action.

In this paper, I want to raise and discuss briefly the question of whether or not the language used in description and explanation of human action is essentially moral language. It will be argued below that the situation can best be described as a continuum of kinds of discourse, rather than by assuming a strict dichotomy between moral language and morally neutral (or 'scientific') language. In short, the language we employ in describing and explaining human action is not —or need not be—essentially moral language, as some writers have thought.

A. I. Melden, for example, holds that 'the concepts "action" and "moral agent" or "person" are . . . correlative.'[1] He notes further: 'We are enabled to participate in the use of discourse by which we impute responsibility to individuals when we treat them as persons or moral agents and their bodily movements as actions.'[2] Melden is representative of those writers who hold that in referring to the actions of persons 'we impute to the individual our common moral form of life.' Thus, on this view, the reporting and describing of human actions 'does *not* employ the neutral language of those concerned to relate or describe bodily movements.'[3] Another writer who makes similar claims is A. R. Louch. He writes: 'To identify a piece of behavior as an action is already to describe experience by means of moral concepts.'[4] And further: 'Talk about human institutions and practices is already a moral cutting of the empirical cake.'[5] Although there is a sound point underlying remarks such as these —namely, that persons frequently act as moral agents and that many actions are subject to moral review— it is a mistake to construe the point as one about the *language* of actions. It is this feature of the accounts of Melden and others that has led them to view the concept of action as *essentially* a moral concept, with the attendant views that subsumption under general laws is impossible and, hence, we cannot speak of causes of action and that therefore, genuine actions are essentially *free* actions. But it would seem that our ability to provide alternative descriptions of actions shows, at the very least, that the language of actions is not essentially moral language.

There is an additional point concerning the context in which any action may occur, which has engendered some confusion. That is, it is often pointed out that a context can be supplied in which an action that might otherwise appear innocent or morally neutral becomes subject to moral review. Thus the action of rubbing my eyebrow with my thumb appears morally neutral when described out of context or in most ordinary contexts. But if rubbing my eyebrow with my thumb is an agreed upon signal which sets into motion a plot to assassinate the Generalissimo, then a context exists in which the action is subject to moral review. Now some writers have thoughts that the actual existence of such contexts or our ability to supply them artificially (for the purpose of philosophical example) shows that there is an inextricable link between action concepts and morality. However, it seems that these considerations show only that human actions (or, more strictly, bodily movements) are performed in a variety of situations, only *some* of which are appropriately viewed as moral contexts when they occur in real life. So the view that actions are, in principle, subject to moral review since a context can always be supplied which makes moral categories relevant is beside the point. For the very contextual factors which lead us, in some actual cases, to judge that moral categories are relevant, would lead us, in other cases, to judge the action as morally neutral (e.g., rubbing my eyebrow with my thumb in most ordinary circumstances).

It is generally agreed that actions do not 'present themselves' nor are they 'given' to an observer in the sense that only one description of the actions will or must be uniquely applicable. The same point can be made concerning the agent; that is, he may view the action he is performing as falling under various alternative descriptions. This is a crucial feature of the concept of action and is relevant to the epistemological questions of understanding and explaining actions. Thus, the following principle appears to be true:

> Actions admit of various alternative descriptions, all of which may be true of the action, and no one of which need be uniquely applicable.

To say that a description is true of an action is merely to say that the action *does* have the features imputed to it, or that one way in which the action can be correctly understood is in terms of its features falling under that description.

There is a related, but somewhat different point concerning a viewer's perception of an action. In perceiving an event as an action, different persons may pick out different features as constitutive of the action in question. Or the same person may, at different times, select certain features rather than others, in perceiving an action. There is, consequently, a possibility of different perceptions of the same action, and no one of these perceptions is privileged or more 'natural' than any other. There may be various ways in which a given action may be seen or viewed, all of which may be equally natural. This latter point is a psychological one, relating to differences among viewers or differences in the same viewer from one time to another. The former point, concerning the descriptions of actions, is a logical point about the concept of action. Insofar as the present concern is with the language of actions, the concentration will be on the issue of alternative descriptions of actions, rather than on the psychological issue of different perceptions or views of the same action. The psychological issue is of some importance, however, when we approach the problem of picking out relevant features in attempting to understand an action or in subjecting it to moral review. That is, for certain purposes we may have, or for our interests at the moment (e.g., explanation, moral praise or blame), some ways of viewing an action may be more appropriate than other ways.

A similar point can be made about descriptions of actions. Although it is true that one description which can be given of an action is the description it bears for the agent (perhaps several descriptions), it still may be the case that *other* descriptions which can be given are also true of the action and, hence, applicable to it. This is not a trivial point,

F

for although in many cases alternative descriptions of actions are equally applicable, this is not always the case. To be sure, it makes no essential difference whether we describe a particular action as 'signing a legal document' or as 'appending one's signature to a deed'; or, in the case of someone driving a car, if we say 'raising one's arm' or 'signaling.' But there are cases in which the descriptions we give of an action—whether or not the action bears that description for the agent—may be of crucial importance. By way of example, two kinds of cases can be cited, one which is relevant to moral evaluation and the other which is relevant to our complete understanding of the agent's action in some psychological sense. In the first kind of case, it makes a great deal of difference whether an action is described as 'lighting a fire' or as 'committing arson.' Similarly, it makes a difference whether or not an action is described as 'writing a letter to Jones' or as 'blackmailing Jones.' In these cases, the alternative descriptions are true of the action so that no one description is *uniquely* applicable. It might be objected that whenever moral evaluation is at issue, some descriptions are *more* applicable than others, and this seems like a plausible view although it cannot simply be assumed, but must be argued for. In any case, it will make a great deal of difference both for our moral evaluation of actions and for our ability to formulate general psychological laws, whether actions are described in morally neutral terms or in terms which are themselves normative.

The second kind of case mentioned above is that in which the descriptions given of an action place it in an entirely different light with respect to our understanding (perhaps 'deep' understanding) or our ability to explain the action. Such is the case with many psychological or Freudian accounts which, in providing alternative descriptions of an action, may change our interpretation of the action (of course, the provision of such descriptions is only as good as the theory behind them). Thus we may describe an action in the following way: 'Jones was rude to his boss'; or alternatively: 'Jones was acting out his hostility to his father.' Or, in another case: 'Smith married a matronly older woman,' described by a psychiatrist as 'Smith exhibited his repressed desire for his mother.' It is true that the second statement in each of these cases is an 'interpretive' statement, rather than one which is 'purely descriptive.' But this is only to say that the interpretive statements have theoretical import, whereas the purely descriptive ones do not. The point here is that all of these statements correctly describe the actions in question (given the correctness of the underlying theory, in the latter cases) and it cannot be maintained that only one description is uniquely applicable. Thus it is not the case that the description which an action bears for the agent is the uniquely applicable description, or even the most applicable one, in all cases. Psychoanalytic or other psychological statements may provide us with a deeper understanding of the action in question, even if the agent does not at first (or, perhaps, ever) assent to such descriptions which his action might bear.

A Skinnerian might make a similar point, claiming that a redescription of a piece of behavior in terms of stimuli, operants, and respondents is always possible, in principle, and that such redescriptions would afford us with greater explanatory and predictive power due to the greater systematization involved. In this case, action-events or pieces of behavior are related to classes of behavior emitted by the organism.

It is apparent that many actions can be described using *either* morally neutral terms, or those which are laudatory or condemnatory. Writers such as Melden and Louch link the concept of action itself with praise or blame. But as we have seen, with respect to the descriptions of many actions, moral terms are inapplicable or irrelevant. The position of those writers who make the link between action and morality forces them into propounding a freewill thesis which they take to be a necessary consequence of their position. This involves a denial on their part that determinism is true, or that it can be applied to human action, a result which is consistent with their claims that we cannot speak of the causes of human action. But if we attend, once again, to the alternative descriptions which can be given of actions, noting that the same action can be alternatively described using morally neutral terms or laudatory and condemnatory terms, we are likely to find that it is under the morally neutral descriptions that we can give causal explanations of human action. Whatever general laws (psychological or sociological) are now available or might someday be discovered, it is likely that they will be couched in morally neutral terms. Even our commonsense generalizations reflect this. We do not say: 'Anyone with a starving family who has no means of livelihood will go out and steal food for his family'; but rather, something like: 'Anyone with a starving family who has no means of livelihood will attempt, by some means or other, to procure food for his family.' An instantiation of the latter generalization may be, under one description, an instance of stealing food. But the generalization (whether universal or statistical in form) need not be of the former sort in order to subsume the particular case under it. Thus we may never —and it is a mistake to suppose that we must—have psychological laws which essentially involve *moral* terms. But we may have more general behavioral laws whose various instantiations might, *under other descriptions,* involve moral terms.

It seems to be the view of Melden and others that all action terms are essentially moral, a result (among other factors) which leads them to deny the possibility of giving causal explanations of human action. But once we see that actions may be subsumed under some more plausible psychological laws, under descriptions which are morally neutral, then we can expect that causal explanations of human action will be provided under these latter sorts of descriptions which do not entail a linguistic commitment to freewill. Under some descriptions of an action the notion of moral responsibility may be inapplicable. And if the concept of responsibility is inapplicable, then so is the concept of freewill. Determinism, then, can be construed in this context as the thesis that under *some* relevant description of the action in question, we can cite a cause or causes. This may be a weak version of the deterministic thesis, but it may be all that the thesis deserves or requires. In addition, it may become more important as psycho-physiological theory becomes more advanced. For, the more correlations that are found to obtain between physiological (*e.g.,* neurological) events or states, and various mental events or states, the more plausible determinism might become (although it still need not entail a mechanistic view of human action).

The question of freewill or freedom only properly arises when the action is described in moral terms or in a context where the question of praise or blame is apposite, even if the action is described in morally neutral terms. That is, the concept of freedom is only applicable where the notion of moral responsibility is applicable.[6] Although the notions of responsibility and freedom may be inapplicable in some contexts and applicable in others, the question of providing psychological laws is never inapplicable, under some description which might be given of the action. The conclusion is that we may be able to provide causal laws under which some descriptions of the action can be subsumed, but not others (*i.e.* those which involve moral terms). If determinism is true, then to call an action free is to say that it is caused in some way or **ways** rather than other ways (*e.g.* it does not come about as a result of external compulsion or duress, or internal psychological compulsion). Accordingly, we need to talk of *action-descriptions* when raising questions of understanding, explanation, moral evaluation, and the like. The popular and overworked distinctions between actions and bodily movements and between what a person *does* and what *happens* to him[7] are a result of oversimplification. Rather, it seems that the distinctions should be made along a continuum of action-descriptions or, better, human-event-descriptions. At one end of the continuum are those descriptions of bodily movements and physiological or neurological occurrences which clearly admit of causal explanations. At the other end of the continuum are those descriptions of actions or of what a person does which essentially involve moral terms and to which the concepts of freewill, responsibility, and praise and blame are clearly applicable. It should be noted that of the various true descriptions that can be given of a particular action-event, alternative descriptions may be applicable all along this continuum. Of all the descriptions which are true of a particular action-event, only under some of these descriptions will we be able to provide causal explanations. This is because providing a causal explanation is furnishing an explanation *under a given description*. It is not to say that the action itself is not caused, but simply that some descriptions of an action are not candidates for subsumption under causal laws.

Viewed as a continuum along which action-descriptions can be given, the problematic area lies in the middle, where motive concepts and emotion concepts are typically employed. It is precisely here that the question of causes versus reasons has arisen with respect to the type of explanation which can be given. But seen as facing both ways—toward the neuro-physiological end of the continuum and towards the moral end—this middle area becomes less problematic. A mistake made by many recent writers on action seems to be that of assuming that the possibility of giving causal explanations of actions would entail that such explanations must be possible or applicable under any descriptions whatever. But this is to oversimplify the concept of action and to link actions inextricably with the moral-description end of the continuum.

To claim, therefore, that causal explanations of human action are possible is not to say that such explanations can be given *under any description* of actions. It is to say that there are descriptions of action-events that can be given—and not merely physiological or neurological descriptions which allegedly apply only to 'bodily movements'—which, when subsumed under the appropriate psychological laws, enable us to answer the question 'Why did X do A?' by giving the causes of his action.

Notes and References

1. 'Action,' *Essays in Philosophical Psychology*, Donald F. Gustafson (ed.). (Garden City, N.Y.: Doubleday and Co., 1964), p. 73.

2. *Ibid.*, p. 74.
3. *Ibid.*, p. 75.
4. *Explanation and Human Action* (Berkeley and Los Angeles: University of California Press, 1966), p. 4.
5. *Ibid.*, p. 171.
6. It might be objected that the term 'freedom' and its cognates are being construed somewhat narrowly here. It is true that I am not employing the term in one ordinary sense in which it denotes a metaphysical category. Indeed, my remarks here are to be construed as a recommendation for using terms like 'free will' and 'free' in a way that bypasses many of the traditional problems, yet retains an important sense of the terms—a sense which is relevant to notions of moral responsibility and other moral categories.
7. For a discussion of these distinctions and their importance for a theory of action, see my 'Doing and Happening,' *Review of Metaphysics*, Vol. XXII (1968).

Ethics and Uniformity

JAMES T. KING
Northern Illinois University

1. Uniformity, a postulate of ethics

For the most part contemporary moral theorists have taken for granted
a uniformity of norm-subjects, and have attended to the logic of moral
language operating under the unquestioned assumption that moral subjects are in the requisite respects alike. Writing in a year fertile for moral
philosophy, the French philosopher Levy-Bruhl[1] faced this question
squarely and concluded that moral theory[2] with its universal or general
norms is simply illegitimate. Levy-Bruhl stated that belief in the uniformity of human nature (the phraseology is his) is the first of two
postulates for moral theory, neither of which is logically tenable. He
takes this postulate to require that human nature is somehow the
same throughout time and space. We may supplement this by saying
that the requirements of uniformity vary from context to context, but
that basically the uniformity postulate of ethics may be taken to mean
that the respects in which individuals are subject to moral norms, or
represent what these norms are meant to preserve and protect, are
respects uniformly realized in all human beings.

That Levy-Bruhl was correct in claiming some Principle of Uniformity of Human Nature (henceforth, PUHN) to be a postulate of
ethics because (a) ethics formulates general rules, and (b) ethics assumes
but does not prove that the collectivity represented by the tag, 'human
nature,' is a collectivity of uniform norm-subjects.

Regarding (a), little need be said. As respected a moral philosopher
as Kurt Baier stipulates that the moral point of view 'must be thought
of as a standpoint from which rules are considered as being acted on
by everyone.'[3] Whereas this condition is formalized by Kant as a demand for universalizability, empirically-leaning philosophers (like

Hume, who affirms that morality consists in general rules)[4] have been led from a different direction to a parallel conclusion. Though schemes of action (or existential 'life projects') which embody no suggestion of generalizations are conceivable, they would scarcely qualify as moral theories. A moral theory must have some generalization techniques, however parsimonious and circumspect, and will to some extent subscribe to the PUHN.

This is not to suggest that the PUHN is an arbitrary or unfounded postulate. Indeed, mature persons with a broad education are commonly of the opinion that we are all one mankind and that in the face of this conception of Humanity, our idiosyncrasies and differences evaporate into unimportance. On the other hand, there are good reasons to question the validity of the PUHN as a postulate for ethics.

2. Is the uniformity principle supported by facts?

In 1903 Levy-Bruhl debunked the notion of an abstract or ideal 'human nature continuously self-identical at every time and place.'[5]
He reasoned that:

1) Every definite abstract-ideal notion of 'Man' is historically conditioned and consequently mirrors the prejudices and leanings of the age, class or individual who elaborated it.[6]

2) Since anthropological studies have displayed the limitless variance of beliefs and practices among societies and since psychological studies have manifested amazingly diverse individual typologies, the abstract notion of 'Man' is wholly untenable, artificial, impoverished.[7]

3) Even if the sciences someday reach a stage of achievement at which precise empirical content can be given to the general notion 'Man,' that notion would not itself possess normative functions or direct normative implications.[8]

I take it that these familiar arguments refute the claims that (1) we have at our disposal some useful abstract or ideal notion of human nature and (2) that this general notion serves as the basis for general rules of conduct (*e.g.,* rules conforming with the powers or demands of 'human nature'). Since the view against which Levy-Bruhl argued has fallen into disuse today, and so we need not dwell on this abstract attempt to justify the uniformity postulate.

Rejection of a self-identical 'human nature' still leaves open (indeed, makes more relevant) the question whether there is or is not, *as a matter of fact,* a sufficient uniformity among people that we may now affirm that generalization in ethics is a valid, feasible procedure. It is noteworthy that on a factual approach the question of uniformity or disuniformity is in principle empirically verifiable or resolvable. Moreover, it is a prima facie legitimate question, perhaps in its colloquial forms ('Are people really alike?' or 'Do we really have very much in common?') even a fairly frequent question in our times. Some answer, I submit, can and should be given to this question.

De facto uniformity among norm-subjects in the context of general moral rules means that:

1) all or nearly all the norm-subjects are capable (whatever the cost) of abiding by the rule (*ought* implies *can*);

2) no norm-subject inculpably fails to share the belief that the norm-target is sufficiently undesirable to warrant modification of any and everyone's actions along the lines dictated by the norm;

3) the cost of norm-abidance will represent roughly the same tolerability for all, or nearly all, norm-subjects.

I append a few aids to interpretation of these conditions for a factual uniformity claim. First, norm-subjects are all those for whom the norm-giving authority intends the norms. Second, in (1), 'all or nearly all' makes room for negligible exceptions; the quantity of exceptions that is considered negligible will decrease as the undesirability of the norm-target increases. Further, in condition (2) the term 'inculpably' is to be interpreted by men acknowledged for good sense and good will; in (3), 'roughly the same tolerability' is to be interpreted by any mature individual for his own case.

When the uniformity postulate is presented as a factual claim, however, moral philosophy itself presents two all-too-common facts suggesting that the requisite uniformity is not available to support the having in ethics of rules meant for everyone. First, it is a fact that moral rules are frequently broken; if moral rules were based on a uniform condition of norm-subjects, uniform norm-abidance should be expected to ensure. But in addition to the fact of common nonabidance we have the nonabiders' accounts of their reasons for disconforming to moral rules. These usually take the form either that abidance imposes an intolerable burden, or that a desire or motive to act in some fashion other than that dictated by the norm outweighed reasons for abiding. In other words, nonabidance is explained in terms of factors that directly counter conditions (2) and (3) stated above. Furthermore, some norm-abiders affirm that, if it were not the case that sanctions are attached to rules, they would not abide by these rules at all. Thus, not only is there insufficient uniformity among people to generate norm-abidance on the part of nearly all subjects, but even what abidance is avilable at a given time in a society is not accounted for solely by uniformity of agents as norm-subjects, but rather by this plus the (uniform) motive of sanction-avoidance.

The second argument against the uniformity postulates is this. If it be thought that the uniformity of human nature is somehow an important or vital support for ethics, it should be pointed out that human nature appears, on this factual approach, more uniformly nonmoral or immoral than it appears moral. This is quite evident if one keeps in mind that 'being moral' is not, according to most philosophers, merely a matter of being human. Rather, one may *become* moral if one takes certain steps (acts on the 'good will,' is sensitive to sympathy, makes a commitment, is rational, or what have you). There seem to be, however, other points or view or motivational frameworks *more* common, *more* natural and closer to the condition of *uniformity* among people than is the moral point of view. One of these is, in the opinion of most moral philosophers, sharply opposed to morality. This factual observation regarding self-interest being *more common* than the moral point of view, would seem to suggest that men in general, if anything are more uniformly amoral or immoral than they are moral.

To this line of reasoning it might be objected along familiar Kantian lines that morality lies not in what is done, but concerns what ought to be done; and hence that morality need not be connected with the ordinary motives of human actions. It is difficult to see what sense this objection might make. It certainly cannot stem from the view that the factual uniformity or disuniformity of human nature is irrelevant to morality, for there can be no general moral rules unless there is something (if it be only practical reason) common to men. To say that generalization regarding what ought to be done is legitimate means that it makes sense to ascribe duties to norm-subjects simply because they are human beings (or something of the sort); and this will make sense only if some relevant respect or characteristic is realized in all these norm-subjects (ascribees of duty). Generally ascribing something to-be-done in turn makes sense only if there is generally some motive that can really induce norm-abiding action. Accordingly, introducing the ought factor does not modify our problem, for the ought may be generalized only if there is, as a matter of *fact,* some 'ought-receptive' uniformity among the ought-subjects.[9]

3. Objective uniformity: A postulate for the sciences and for history

Uniformity of human nature is relevant to cognitive endeavors other than moral philosophy. In the sciences of Man and in the presuppositions of History there is some reliance on a principle of uniformity of human nature. Perhaps moral philosophy may lean on these elaborations for its own purposes, 'borrowing,' in other words, from the established concepts of related disciplines.

There are scientific disciplines which have as the object of their inquiry human phenomena and which issue fairly respectable general laws or theories showing people to be uniform in certain respects. Proceeding from positive observations to the formulation of general laws or empirical regularities relative to human beings, social scientists have succeeded in giving some content to the notion of a uniformity of human nature. Thus, although moral theory may not be able to establish the PUHN through its methods, by following the PUHN as it is validated by the sciences, moral theory may be able to obtain a ground for its generalizations. Such, by the way, is roughly Levy-Bruhl's own expectation about the future of moral theory.

That in principle some project like this is feasible I find it hard to doubt, and yet there are good reasons to wonder whether moral theorists would be willing to accept the strictures of scientific method and the possible infringement upon the autonomy of ethics (as they see it). If our earlier remarks are not misplaced, furthermore, there is no guarantee that the scientifically respectable set of general propositions about Man will not comprise elements opposed to the moral point of view, such as the facts of self-interest, exploitation, bad faith, and so on. It is not inconceivable that such findings would block any factual support for the PUHN as moral theorists would utilize it.

The phenomena which history claims to explain (insofar as they may be accounted for) are basically the same as those which concern the moral theorist, namely, human actions. Whether the historian appeals to environmental and motivational causes or whether to the historical agent's deliberate reasons, his account of human actions succeeds pretty much to the extent that, in addition to satisfying the canons of historical evidence, it makes plausible sense to us. This description of the historian's procedures ultimately gives place, however, either to a suggestion of a 'transcendental illusion' or to the postulation of some form of PUHN. If the demand that a historian's account of an action in the past appeal to explanatory factors seeming plausible to us today be read as an illegitimate projection in the past of our own frameworks of motives and/or reasons, then certainly the putative explanation is no more than a logical illusion. On the other hand, if we can honestly *learn* from history, it must be the case that between the past actions which are the historian's *explananda* and our historical situations there is some degree of continuity. Who acknowledges the successes of historical explanation leans on and underwrites a uniformity postulate to some extent—although he probably has for such a postulate little rigorous evidence outside the fact that this is a pre-supposition of an enterprise which he deems worthwhile and which is generally acknowledged as successful. This *probatur ambulando* justification of some form of uniformity postulate in the context of historical explanation might be thought to be provisionally adoptable by the moral theorist (giving an ethics somewhat like Hobbes') until a more rigorous scientific content is accorded the notion of human nature. The moral theorist might thus affirm that there is sufficient uniformity of human nature that we can understand the causes and reasons for one another's actions—in other words, in respect of the intelligibility of their actions, human beings are uniform (or nearly so).

Now there seem to be serious reasons why a scientific or historical conception of a uniformity of human nature will not serve as a sufficient support for moral generalization.

1) The human sciences reveal at least as much disuniformity as they do uniformity.

2) If moral theory takes over conclusions reached through scientific methodology, it may come to be more restricted and cramped than it would be relying solely on its own procedures.

3) As Levy-Bruhl argued, the conclusions of science, while relevant to moral theory, are of themselves not normative. The groundwork of moral theory is autonomous and independent of the sciences—though its conclusions are not wholly so.

4) Moreover, the human sciences, and history particularly, show that factors relating to immorality—such as self-interest, exploitation, bad faith, and so on—are as intelligible and perhaps even more widespread and uniform than those relating to morality.

5) It is by no means clear that even the most astute moral philosopher

could find in the historian's postulate of a uniformity of human nature a satisfactory support for moral generalizations. The drawbacks of generalizing moral rules, when balanced against the historian's reliance on the postulate, may considerably outweigh in significance whatever evidence for uniformity is derivable from that discipline.

These difficulties suggest the conclusion that a uniformity postulate is not sufficiently established and amplified in the human sciences or as a presupposition of historical explanation to afford the requisite backdrop for the more interesting instances of generalization in ethics. Perhaps supplementary support might be derived from pragmatic considerations and straightforward common sense.

5. Objective uniformity: an assumption for policy and decision-making

In ordinary matters of policy-determination and decision-making we usually cannot proceed long without relying on some belief in a uniformity of human nature. Individuals make decision relative to persons whom they do not know well or at all, decisions of moment and importance. No sensitive decision-maker will permit himself to touch the lives of other persons if he had no idea how the action in question will be received by the parties affected by it. Hence, either this typical decision-maker should rely on some acceptable generalization about people, or he should refrain from action until he ascertains and weighs in the balance the attitudes, likes and dislikes, long-range goals, *etc.*, of all the parties to be affected by the decision.

While there are cases in which the sensitive decision-maker must obtain full detailed knowledge of the attitudes of the parties affected (*e.g.*, the disposition of children in divorce cases), we feel it would be unreasonable to place such requirements on all decision-making generally, since by that token much action would be brought to a standstill. On the whole it seems fair to say that many general policies, informed by the available general findings of the human sciences, are useful and work well. It is noteworthy that, should there be no determinable uniformity among people, this would not cancel out our making or having general policies, for in that case we should all the more need decisions to bring about a minimum of uniformity (despite differences of opinion or attitude) requisite for some form of social coexistence.

As a matter of fact, however, having general policies and acting on a tacit assumption of uniformity, is a successful and effective way of dealing with people. We are able to formulate general policy because we often know what the vast majority of people want (*e.g.* reduced taxes) and how they will react to scenes or situations (*e.g.* advertising decisions are determined by such generalities). Moreover, in our common dealings with people we claim to adjust, learn and advance in experience because what we come to know through trial-and-error in earlier experiences we take to be applicable (*mutatis mutandis*) to different persons and situations later. And naturally this process would fail if there were not in fact some continuity or uniformity among people. Pragmatically, some form of uniformity postulate is convalidated in our individual and corporate action on general policies, beliefs and expectations. These successes, be it noted, would automatically be cancelled if our actions met with significant opposition or dissent. Such, it seems, is the gist of a *probatur ambulando* justification of reliance on an assumption of uniformity in prudential matters and policy-making. If the uniformity postulate is flatly denied, general rules, policies or expectations must be considered irrational, or at least illegitimate.

Let us now suppose that we can collect from the presuppositions and findings of the human sciences, of history and of our intelligent social experience the totality of true statements holding of all or nearly all people which may be said to be relevant to moral theory. Thus content will be given to the conception of uniformity of human nature. The question then is: of what use to moral theory is such a concept?

First, insofar as such a conception holds of all or nearly all people, it gives the moral agent information necessary to answer the question: how should people be treated? Objective uniformity regarding what are universal preferences is indeed morally relevant and affords a solid support for some moral generalizations. But precisely because they are so general, these considerations do not reliably hold in all or nearly all cases requiring action in a moral situation, for: (1) it is no guarantee that action in a specific case will be right or approvable merely because *action of this sort* represents a uniform or general preference; and (2) there may be some uniform or general human preferences which as it turns out, do not represent what is morally preferable or right. Hence it is possible that even with this comprehensive conception of uniform human nature, there is not afforded to moral theory a justification of the strategies of universalization or of generalizing moral rules. Nevertheless, an understanding of objective uniformity of human nature is welcome in moral theory—ethics would limp without it.

A stronger interpretation of the relevance of objective uniformity would identify it with morality. Should it be granted that there is a number of uniform preferences (*e.g.* not to be slain, not to be embarrassed, *etc.*), it might be affirmed with some plausibility that morality consists in the sum of these uniform preferences. On such a view, however, two perhaps unwelcome consequences would result. First, what is morally right and wrong would be determinable by nose-counting. And second, morality would become trite, for what are universal (or nearly so) preferences are by definition rather well known to us all. Such a morality would be little more than the expression of *what people already want* (uniformly).

We seem to have come to an impasse. Either moral theory is naturalistic (and accordant with some factual uniformity claim) but is reduced to triteness, or moral theory is interestingly normative (but turns its back on factual disuniformity of human nature) and is thus a questionable enterprise. I take it that so long as we are philosophizing about and with facts (or fact-claims), we shall not avoid this dilemma—and accordingly Levy-Bruhl's attack on the uniformity postulate of normative ethics should thus far be considered unimpeachable.

6.   Normative ethics and desirable uniformity

Yet these conclusions are thoroughly unacceptable. Ethics is not a restatement of what people uniformly do or believe, but rather is rational discourse about what practices are right and good—specifically, discourse about what practices and attitudes it is desirable should become uniform among people. Uniformity is not so much a postulate as a desideratum of ethics. Hence, the idea that moral rules are meant for everybody should be interpreted to mean not that everybody already wants what these rules stand for, but that it is desirable that what these rules stand for become a uniform practice. Uniformity is morality's goal, not its starting-point.

Two objections immediately spring to mind. First, it might be objected that uniformity itself is undesirable and odious. We imagine the faceless 'mass man' of 1984, dweller in a metaphorical society of anthropoids all stamped from the same machine (*etc.*). Against this we react, relishing variety, creativity, novelty, freedom, individuality. We refuse to say that morality resides in what it is desirable to bring about as a uniform practice because uniformity is, we think, simply undesirable.

The second objection affirms that the bringing about of uniform practices among people who are not uniform is impossible without tyranny and oppression. In my opinion, both objections can be met; I shall consider the latter first.

The point of the objection that uniformity of practice cannot be had when people are not uniform is not so much a logical as a moral one, namely that compulsion and oppression of dissidents is wrong, or is undesirable to a greater degree than uniformity may be desirable. This moral point is, I affirm, a valid one, but it impugns not the notion that uniformity is desirable, but the notion that uniformity through compulsion is desirable. I should also affirm that uniformity through compulsion is wrong and undesirable, but still say that it is possible to bring about uniformity (the uniformity that it is rationally desirable there should be in society) by non-oppressive means, principally through discourse, persuasion and dialogue. I declare my conviction that uniformity through non-oppressive means is possible, and I do so fully aware of contemporary social violence and cynicism. To argue the point seriously, however, would require another paper. My thesis boils down to this: there are completely rational 'uniformity-generating' agencies which may be tapped in efforts to maximize agreement on what it is desirable to bring about as a uniform practice in society. If these are successfully employed, uniformity will ensue without repression and tyranny.

The first objection is inconsistent, first because proponents of freedom and variety acknowledge that it is desirable that some practices become uniform in society, nonmurdering, for example. And further because the conditions of life in defense of which they speak out— freedom, creativity, individuality, and so on—are conditions which they deem it desirable should be uniform in society. The objection seems to be levelled not against uniformity as such, but against forced or mindless uniformity.

I do not expect this response to satisfy every upholder of individuality; there are misanthropes, recluses, againsters, hermits and other assorted individualists for whom in general what is socially desirable means little or nothing. These parties who give little to social well-being but ask little from society are, in my opinion, living an impoverished life; yet it is undeniable they should be permitted to withdraw from the cooperative social enterprise and to their separate ways, undisrupted and undisrupting. They are the exceptions.

Should an objector assert finally that considerations of freedom and unhampered individuality simply override considerations of what it is desirable to bring about as a uniform practice in society (even nonmurdering, for example), then the objector should be informed that societies do not recognize freedom to commit certain acts, and will not tolerate them. I do not know how else such an objector might be answered. If a man claims that murdering is alright, all we can do is tell him he is wrong and try to show him why.

For the remainder of us values of a different sort are paramount: amity, understanding, agreement and cooperativeness are not only desirable, but are absolutely and immediately right. They mark the achievement by rational individuals of the fullness of the conditions that enrich human life.

That amity and cooperativeness, for example be recognized as immediately and absolutely right, it is requisite that one consider *other people* to be of great worth (respected as ends, acknowledged to have dignity, *etc.*). Unless this condition is realized, amity and cooperativeness will be simply uninteresting or undesirable. The moral point of view differentiates respecting other people as ends, *i.e.* holding human beings as objects of rational esteem, on the one hand, from disinterest and disconcern for other people, on the other hand.

It is vital to recognize, accordingly, that from the moral point of view human nature *is* uniform in a very significant way. This is a uniformity of worth—people are uniformly to be treated as ends. In this context, however, uniformity figures not as a fact or as a postulate, but as the basic principle of morality, an expression of what is distinctive about the moral point of view. Relative to the *facts,* nevertheless, it would seem that the moral point of view oversteps the limits of strict evidence insofar as it deems all human beings to have worth independent of their individual merit or dismerit. It is particularly noteworthy that, whereas moral theory illegitimately oversteps the limits of the evidence insofar as it presupposes factual uniformity among norm-subjects (and even norm-objects), on the other hand the moral point of view felicitiously is not limited to the facts in asserting human beings to be uniformly of unique worth. The former overextension deserves to be emended; the latter does not. I contend that the problem of ethics and uniformity is not properly understood unless this distinction is kept in view.

There is a tension between the uniform worth of human beings and their factual disuniformity. Emphasizing this worth at the expense of generalized rules or principles gives a lazy ethics whose sole principle and content is tolerance. The overly familiar 'Do your own thing' is all that remains of ethics if disuniformity is accepted as a terminal fact. Regardless of the significance of the comprehensive (scientific and pragmatic) concept of uniform human nature (which would show that ob-

jective disuniformity should not be accepted as a fact), this content-
less ethics is not interesting or moral, for the fullness of human life is
found in social coexistence, and the moral point of view culminates
in the notion of community, amity and cooperativeness. Systematically
acting on no principle at all is inimical to community, amity and co-
operation because it maximizes the disuniformity factor, and uniformity
is a condition of community (and to some extent a measure of it). It
is precisely in the respect that the moral point of view aims at community and amity that uniformity may be said to be a *desideratum*
of ethics.

There is another way of seeing the tension between uniformity as a
desideratum of ethics and disuniformity as a fact, namely, which should
yield to the other? Should we concentrate on adjusting the scope of
ethical generalizations to suit the facts, specifically, the actual amounts
and degrees of uniformity and disuniformity we have in our society; or
should we aim at minimizing the disuniformity by implementing
available 'uniformity-generating' means, so as to effect agreement and
unanimity? For the most part the latter alternative is open and when
so, for rational men it seems the only worthy alternative.

7.   Means of generating uniformity

On several occasions I have mentioned uniformity-generating agencies.
By this I mean courses of action or social processes whereby amity,
understanding, and cooperativeness are fostered. These means facilitate
agreement and show how it is that to a very important extent we are
all alike.

1. Acculturalization increases for the individual the number of beliefs,
attitudes, experiences, evaluations, *etc.* he has in common with the other
members of his society. One of the jobs that a culture does is to
provide a cognitive-affective backdrop for community; a culture exists
by being held in common. As individuals become acculturalized, they
come to have more in common with other people—we become, in this
respect, alike.

2. Through communication and especially conversation the individual
cannot help but have his horizon broadened by the viewpoint of others.
The incommunicative person is unlikely to enter into the sharing relationships by which we grow alike.

3. When people are warm, open, amicable, understanding, they effuse

these qualities and often immediately affect others by their contagious contact, or at least awaken in others a wish to be like them. As we become more sensitive, either in contrived training sessions or by reacting to the warmth of others, we come to realize that we are all basically alike—all human.

4. It is in the very nature of a rational conviction to be based on general reasons which its holder believes should be universally accepted, and of which he is impelled to try to convince others. If rational inquiry and dialogue be permitted to develop amply in time, unanimity is more likely to ensue than might be expected through any other means.

5. Finally, there is the moral point of view, to which nearly everyone subscribes to some extent at least. The thrust of morality and of humanistic education is directed, I submit, at reason and understanding, amity and cooperativeness. As the moral point of view becomes more prevalent and effectual, either through trial-and-error or through contagion and dialogue, a unity of mankind gradually comes about, and the uniformity of humanity in respect of worth passes from ideal to actual existence.

I add two brief notes. These uniformity-generating factors tend to balance and reinforce one another. Also, the uniformity they generate is not an indefinite or global uniformity, but uniformity-in-respects. If successful, they produce not a faceless 'mass man' anthropoid, but a rational community. This, I take it, is what moral philosophers are driving at when they talk about the sort of life we would have if everyone were rational.

8.   Conclusions

Levy-Bruhl was correct in affirming that there is no sufficient factual evidence for uniformity either of norm-subjects or of norm-objects (of such a scope as to warrant universal rules or general rules meant to hold of all human beings). The first conclusion impedes universalization in ethics; the second, the moral point of view itself. We may conclude from this that either universalization in ethics is illegitimate (to a varying extent) or that moral rules are person-relative (and that a description of the persons to whom a rule is relative should be appended to it). If rules are wholly person-relative, however, ethics ceases to be normative (as it has usually been understood to be normative, *i.e.*, with valid general rules) and comes to consist in a list of the norms or attitudes people (the 'persons' in person-relative) already accept.

While it is likely that enforcing general moral rules on everyone in general will be oppressive to non-uniform norm-subjects or norm-objects, on the other hand, having no general rules or policies at all seems to be neither sensible nor feasible. Accordingly, it is incumbent upon rational men to concentrate on generating a uniformity and unanimity among the people in their society, so that what the moral point of view stands for may be made a reality.

It is a mistake, I submit, to affirm that the relation of uniformity to ethics is essentially that of a postulate or precondition; uniformity is rather the *desideratum* of ethics. Furthermore, as a *desideratum* of ethics, uniformity among people is relevant not as a formal prerequisite that its desirability should be satisfied logically; uniformity among people is a *desideratum* because it is, I suggest, the chief goal of morality. Uniformity is a condition for amity and understanding, and is desired as integral to the best and most human way of living, namely, in a sharing community. Our factual lack of uniformity, in conclusion, does not impede ethics—instead it impels ethics.

Notes and References

1. Lucien Levy-Bruhl. *La Morale et la Science des Moeurs* (Paris: Alcan, 1903).
2. Levy-Bruhl discussed 'la morale théorique'; I translate this as moral theory or ethics.
3. Kurt Baier, *The Moral Point of View* (New York: Random House, 1965), 100 f.
4. David Hume, *A Treatise of Human Nature* (Oxford: Clarendon, 1965), 581 ff.
5. Levy-Bruhl, *op. cit.*, 67.
6. *Ibid.*, 68 ff.
7. *Ibid.*, 76, 81.
8. *Ibid.*, 12, 17 ff.
9. Kant seems naively to have believed that there is a uniform 'ought-receptiveness' even in the wrongdoer who is under the sway of some such motive or inclination as self-interest. This person, Kant thought, even while not conforming to duty, recognizes the superiority of the dutiful way and wishes he were such a man as could to his duty. Though perhaps this holds for the weak-willed norm-subject (whom Aristotle discussed), it certainly does not square with the remarks of blatant anti-moralists and brash immoralists who draw attention to themselves in our age. *Cf.* Immanuel Kant, *Fundamental Principles of the Metaphysic of Morals* (Indianapolis: Bobbs-Merrill, 1949), tr. T. K. Abbott, 42.

Ethical Relativism and the Concept of a Moral Judgment

EDWARD M. SAYLES

University of Michigan, Dearborn Campus

I

Philosophical thinking about mind can be initiated within any one of several perspectives. The broadest way in which to classify the perspective adopted in this essay is in terms of major kinds of judgments. I want to consider the concept of a moral judgment, where by 'moral judgment' is meant 'normative moral judgment' as opposed to 'descriptive moral judgment.' And I want specifically to pursue this consideration in the context of a representative discussion of ethical relativism.

I shall in the first place contend that this representative discussion formulates the issue of ethical relativism over against ethical absolutism in an unnecessarily rigid and polarized way. I shall then outline a reformulation of the issue that will have two emphases: (i) a consideration of ways of evaluating the grounds of ethical relativism; and (ii) the development of a concept of a moral judgment that will allow progress toward a satisfactory resolution of the issue. Within the scope of this essay, I can hope to do no more than to take some preliminary steps.

Even relatively limited reflection on ordinary thought and discourse about morality discloses a significant ambiguity regarding the relation of moral judgments to factual judgments. The dependence of moral judgments upon factual judgments is manifested in the common belief that a defensible moral judgment cannot be made without knowledge of certain facts, such facts falling into three classes: (i) general facts regarding human needs, desires, capabilities, and limitations; (ii) general facts regarding moral customs and moral beliefs about appropriate norms and goals: (iii) particular facts of the situation to which a particular moral judgment is addressed. The first and second classes of facts underlie the formulation of moral judgments that evaluate *kinds* of acts as right or wrong; the third class of facts is required to determine whether a given act is to be subsumed under this or that general moral judgment. For example, facts in the first and second classes support the judgment 'Promise breaking is wrong'; facts in the third class are needed to determine whether in a given situation one is confronting a case of promise breaking.

Set over against this view of dependence is the belief that in an essential way moral judgments, conceived of as converging in a self-consistent system of morality, are independent of factual judgments. In sum they reflect a world for all men that never was nor will be. Taken either as indicating an ultimate good or a proximate better, morality is necessarily ideal; and in being ideal it stands apart from the actualities of human existence.

The representation of this ambiguity in the large and general way in which it appears in common thought may serve as point of departure for its more precise representation in a discussion of ethical relativism. The ambiguity is a central concern of the analysis of the concept of a moral judgment toward which this essay aims.

II

Ethical relativism is not a new doctrine, but there is no doubt that its appeal has been considerably enlarged as a consequence of the development of the social sciences in this century. It is frequently espoused, often quite uncritically, by social scientists and others with a serious interest in the social sciences. These facts are significant in understanding how it has come about that representative philosophical discussions of ethical relativism are chiefly concerned to make explicit the position in question and to evaluate it. Evaluations are usually on the side of finding the position inadequately defended. And while such evaluations may explicitly or implicitly support *some kind* of ethical absolutism, they are very far from being self-contained defenses of ethical absolutism.

Ethical relativism may be represented as the thesis that the defense of a normative moral judgment is correctly carried out from the basis of the moral values of the society within which the judgment is made;

and, since there is, as a matter of fact, a multiplicity of sets of moral values (although not necessarily as many sets as societies), there is a multiplicity of legitimate bases for defending moral judgments. The assertion of the thesis implies a denial of the thesis of ethical absolutism; *viz.*, the correct defense of moral judgments is the same for all societies. That there is a multiplicity of sets of moral values is the claim of what is often called sociological relativism; and it is here, of course, that one encounters the relevant discoveries of historians, sociologists, and anthropologists, beginning, perhaps, with Herodotus. The fundamental argument of the ethical relativist appears to be a substitution instance of *modus ponens*: If sociological relativism is true, then ethical relativism is true; sociological relativism has been shown to be true; it follows that ethical relativism is true.

III

Clearly, the argument as stated is open to the criticism that an unwarranted or, at any rate, controversial presupposition underlies the statement of the first premiss; *viz.*, the presupposition that normative judgments of any kind can validly be inferred from wholly factual judgments, that the 'ought' is derivable from the 'is.' But what of the weaker presupposition that *some* set of factual judgments are required for the legitimate support of moral judgments? In the *Nicomachean Ethics*, Aristotle finds it necessary carefully to consider what man is, including what he is capable of and what he believes about himself, before establishing how man ought to conduct himself. Hobbes' moral philosophy has a thesis of psychological egoism as point of departure. The classical utilitarians make a comparable use of psychological hedonism. Many contemporary moral philosophers regard the chief conclusions of Freudian psychology as being relevant to ethics.

A certain reply is easily anticipated. It will be said that the weaker presupposition allows for more than one kind of relevance of factual judgments to moral judgments, including the kind manifested in the stronger presupposition; but rejection of the stronger presupposition is logically compatible with the defense of or allowance for some other kind of relevance. Further, the philosophers cited, and they are typical of moral philosophers in this respect, while presupposing that in some way ethics rests on psychology, also presuppose that the ethical conclusions to which they are led have a universality. Thus, their ethical conclusions are incompatible with ethical relativism.

Even taking this reply into account, the ethical relativist may urge that the recognition of *some kind* of foundational relevance of factual judgments about human nature and belief to moral judgments makes plausible a careful consideration of the data of sociological relativism, or what I should prefer to call, more neutrally, the sociology of moral beliefs. This defense may be enlarged by the point that these data have been drawn from a wide range of contexts studied scientifically. On the other hand, one may ask whether Aristotle's psychology, despite its claim to represent all men, is too much dependent on Aristotle's observations of Greeks; and the accounts of human nature in Hobbes and Bentham and Mill disproportionately reflective of western Europeans.

In any case, one side of the central ambiguity is in evidence; *viz.*, the dependence of moral judgments upon factual judgments. I turn now to the other side; *viz.*, the independence of moral judgments from factual judgments. In his analysis of ethical relativism, W. T. Stace, having reviewed arguments in its favor, none of which he finds adequate, moves to a different position:

> It is time that we turned our attention from the case in favour of ethical relativity [ethical relativism] to the case against it. Now the case against it consists, to a very large extent, in urging that, if taken seriously and pressed to its logical conclusion, ethical relativity can only end in destroying the conception of morality altogether, in undermining its practical efficacy, in rendering meaningless many almost universally accepted truths about human affairs, in robbing human beings of any incentive to strive for a better world, in taking the life-blood out of every ideal and every aspiration which has ever ennobled the life of man.[1]

The central claim of Stace's chief case against ethical relativism, the claim that ethical relativism is incompatible with the correct concept of morality, and, therefore, incompatible with the correct concept of a moral judgment, is subscribed to, explicitly or implicitly, by many empirical philosophers; it cannot be regarded as eccentric. The claim appears to imply that the facts of the sociology of moral beliefs are irrelevant to the issue of establishing ethical relativism. No matter what social scientists discover in this area of inquiry, the issue must be resolved in opposition to ethical relativism and in favor of some sort of ethical absolutism. Indeed, there never was an issue, since the correct conceptual point of departure that attends the discussion of the grounds of moral judgments rules out ethical relativism. Stace writes: 'The work of the anthropologists, upon which ethical relativists seem to rely so heavily, has as a matter of fact added absolutely nothing *in principle* to what has always been known about the variability of moral ideas.'[2] The tradition of thought within which the correct concept of morality is resident has not been ignorant of some significant facts of the sociology of moral beliefs. The concept has accommodated them, but not by way of concluding to ethical relativism.

Stace does make some use of data from the sociology of moral beliefs in a rhetorical way, in order to make the ethical relativist see that he supports a conceptually untenable doctrine. For example, he urges that ethical relativism requires one to conclude 'that cannibalism is right for people who believe in it.'[3] He supposes that the ethical relativist will agree that this conclusion and many others like it really are implied by his doctrine; and that such conclusions, in being utterly unacceptable, will occasion his rejection of the doctrine. It is of interest to note that the rhetorical use of the example does not require that there be people who do practice cannibalism and believe it to be right to do so. Since cannibalism does occur, the natural rhetorical locution is along these lines: 'If you hold ethical relativism to be true, then you must regard cannibalism as morally right for those societies that elect to practice it.' The rhetorical locution would be different if it were believed that no one has practiced or does now practice cannibalism; it might be: 'If you hold ethical relativism to be true, then you would have to regard cannibalism, were it to occur, as morally right for any society that may elect to practice it.' Now it seems to me that there is no persuasive difference between these two locutions. Each serves equally well to dissuade the ethical relativist from a certain extreme interpretation of his position. If I am correct in this estimate, there is here a reinforcement of the point that the argument exemplified by Stace takes the data of the sociology of moral beliefs to be irrelevant to making the case for some form of ethical absolutism.

If the ethical relativist concedes this point to the ethical absolutist, it may be said that what he has conceded is simply that the domain of legitimate moral judgments is no coextensive with the domain of possible or, indeed, actual moral beliefs. Or, put another way, not every kind of act that may be regarded as a morally approvable kind by one society or another is *really* morally approvable. But the ethical relativist may contend that conceding this point is not to concede that the facts of the sociology of moral beliefs have no relevance at all to the establishment and defense of moral judgments.

What sort of relevance they have may be suggested by a rhetorical use of some of these facts by the ethical relativist. Suppose him to say to the ethical absolutist: 'If you hold ethical absolutism to be true, you are not thereby committed to regarding polygamy as morally wrong for those societies that elect to practice it.' On the other hand, if the ethical absolutist had used the example of polygamy instead of cannibalism in his attempt to score a point against the ethical relativist, his likelihood of success would have been reduced. If the ethical absolutist now concedes the ethical relativist's point, it may be said what he has conceded is that within the domain of legitimate moral judgments there exists with regard to each of numerous topics a range of differing moral beliefs compatible with ethical absolutism. Thus, agreement on the moral necessity of regulating human sexual relations is compatible with regarding monogamy as right in one society and polygamy as right in another.

The discussion of ethical relativism has now been turned in a new direction. The facts of the sociology of moral beliefs are to be examined with the aim of deciding whether, despite the obvious diversity of moral beliefs, there is nevertheless a common set of moral presuppositions underlying them. Such presuppositions are often classified as *basic* moral beliefs, in contrast to the moral beliefs that constitute the data assembled by the social sciences and upon which the case for ethical relativism rests. The question of classification is an important one to which I shall return in the last section of this essay. The above point conceded to the ethical relativist by the ethical absolutist must be given a new interpretation in the light of the issue of common moral presuppositions or basic beliefs. Agreement on the moral necessity of regulating human sexual relations is a *prima facie* example of such a presupposition or belief.

Let us suppose for a moment that the ethical relativist and the ethical absolutist can agree on their use of the term 'basic moral belief'; and, further, that they are able to establish the basic moral beliefs that are resident in all societies. Now if it were shown that all societies have the same basic moral beliefs, the ethical relativist presumably would have to acknowledge that his position had been seriously challenged. He could continue to claim that the same basic moral belief admits of differing acceptable manifestations in differing societies, as in the contrast between monogamy and polygamy. But his thesis would be markedly less forceful if it were exhausted in this claim. On the other hand, if it were shown that basic moral beliefs are not the same for all societies, the ethical relativist presumably would regard his position as having been considerably strengthened, if not indisputably established.

What are the implications for ethical absolutism of these two possible outcomes? If basic moral beliefs are not uniform, the ethical absolutist can say, indeed must say, that at least some of them are mistaken or false. The element in his thesis, and in his concept of a moral judgment, of the independence of moral judgments from factual judgments would require this response. But this same element of independence also would require him to acknowledge that, if basic moral beliefs are uniform, his thesis has not been strengthened; this outcome would be superfluous. It may be noted that the ethical relativist, in the defense of his thesis, cannot make use of the possibility of mistaken or false beliefs. For if basic moral beliefs are not uniform, he would regard his thesis as supported; if they are uniform, he has no grounds on which to claim that at least some of them are mistaken or false.

IV

Now I think that one not committed to either ethical relativism or ethical absolutism, as these theses have been represented here, would regard this perspective on the issue as unsatisfactory. It is chiefly unsatisfactory in that it does not allow an unfettered exploration of the facts of the sociology of moral beliefs. Ethical absolutism stands too much apart from these facts; ethical relativism is too much dependent upon them. And it is clear that a certain concept of a moral judgment is the main support of ethical absolutism, and the main ground of its assault upon ethical relativism. A further consideration of the concept of a moral judgment itself may help to prepare a perspective within which the issue can be more satisfactorily defined.

But it is first necessary to raise some questions as to how the data of the sociology of moral beliefs are properly to be dealt with. In doing this, one may initially be guided by C. D. Broad's account of speculative philosophy. 'Its object,' he writes, 'is to take over the results of the various sciences, to add to them the results of the religious and ethical experiences of mankind, and then to reflect upon the whole.'[4] Broad requires that the development of a speculative philosophy take into account the widest possible range of information, and that it accommodate that range with conceptual economy. If one's attention is largely confined to the 'ethical experiences of mankind,' one may hope to develop a *restricted* speculative philosophy; the restriction is one of subject matter, but the goal of conceptual economy is still operative. Within such an undertaking one may identify a place for the data of the sociology of moral beliefs; they are the grounds of speculation. The concern with conceptual economy and concomitant generalization is reflected in the development of a theory regarding what is appropriately absolute and relative in moral judgments.

It is important to stress that the data in question are represented by the social sciences that advance them as sets of beliefs, chiefly about moral standards, but including also, either explicitly or implicitly, beliefs about what is the case. The psychological foundations of classical ethical theories earlier referred to have their counterparts within these sets of beliefs; but in sum they have a lesser range of subject matter than do the data of the sociology of moral beliefs. Thus, in analyzing these data, it is important to distinguish beliefs about what is the case, including beliefs about human nature, from beliefs about what ought to be the case.

The discussion of ethical relativism introduced considerations of beliefs about moral standards at two levels. The primary level is that at which the data typically are presented by the social sciences; this is the level at which contrasts in moral beliefs from one society to another are most conspicuous. Some claims for the existence of beliefs at this level are, to be sure, inferences from non-linguistic acts. For example, a ceremony engaged in by the members of a given culture is taken as evidence for a specifiable set of moral beliefs. But to speak of basic moral beliefs is to refer to another level, that of the presuppositions of the constituents of the primary level.

But here significant questions are encountered. If one speaks of the presuppositions of moral beliefs at the primary level, one may ask whether the presuppositions are themselves objects of belief. If consciously entertained and defended, then, clearly, they are believed. But if not consciously entertained and defended, can it be said that they would be believed if brought to the notice of those whose primary moral beliefs rest on them? The question is important because, as indicated earlier, the issue of ethical relativism over against ethical absolutism is modified when it makes central a consideration of basic moral beliefs rather than primary moral beliefs. The modification is often regarded as bringing about an advantage to the position of ethical absolutism (in some form), since it appears that one can often resolve the clashes at the primary level by showing that it is reasonable to hold that a common set of basic moral beliefs underlies them. Leaving on one side for a moment the question of how inferences to the presuppositions of primary moral beliefs are defensibly carried out, one should be prepared to accommodate the possibility that such presuppositions, on being made explicit, may be rejected or modified by the person initially holding the relevant primary moral beliefs. While the possibility of rejection or modification exists, the sociological 'facts' are subject to revision.

The recognition of moral presuppositions leads one to ask whether there is a hierarchy of presuppositions. The presupposition that it is morally necessary to regulate human sexual relations may be said to entail the wider presupposition that it is morally necessary to order and perpetuate societies (or at least one's own society). It is clear that the issue of ethical relativism requires one to consider elements more fundamental than those constituting the primary level. But it may be doubted that presuppositions at the *most* fundamental level, even if what these are could be agreed upon, provide the most useful context for sharpening the present issue. The relevant level may be that which exhibits beliefs about the rationales of institutions in society. In any case, the concept of a moral judgement must incorporate explicit or implicit reference to the question of this hierarchy.

If it is significant to consider moral presuppositions, it is clearly important to consider how they are to be established. There is need for the development of a method or set of methods appropriate to this task. It is not unreasonable to regard this task as one of reconstructing thought; and the inquirer into the sociological facts pertaining to ethical relativism may discover that the methodological questions he comes to confront may be comparable to those confronted by historians. The work of R. G. Collingwood, among other philosophers of history, may be brought into contact with the present question of the analysis of sociological data. It cannot be claimed that Collingwood developed a satisfactory method for resolving the questions of the reconstruction of thought that he believed historians must ask. But his efforts suggest a way in which the multiplicity or moral standards resident in both the historical dimension and in the dimension of contemporary cultures can be systematically investigated.

As regards the large enterprise of analyzing the data of the sociology of moral beliefs, what questions ought to be posed in order to advance a formulation of the concept of a moral judgment that reflects awareness of the analysis? It is important to determine what beliefs about the nature of the cosmos and about human nature are held or implied by differing societies. Many such beliefs are subject to the critique of the empirical sciences; and, clearly, a responsible ethical theory will insist upon a scientific defense, so far as that is possible, of its cognitive foundations. Of greater significance is the question of what is believed regarding: (i) what kinds of facts are relevant to establishing moral judgments; and (ii) what is the nature of that relevance. Here one encounters the question of justifying moral judgments; and the accompanying question of defending a metaethical position.

The defense of a particular metaethical position obviously has implications for what a moral judgment is taken to be. An illuminating comment on this problem is provided by William Alston, in discussing J. L. Austin's distinctions among locutionary, illocutionary, and perlocutionary acts:

> The analysis of illocutionary acts . . . becomes of crucial importance in ethics. A great deal of ethical theory is concerned with getting clear as to what we are doing when we make moral judgments. We must be clear about this if we are to know what considerations are appropriate for supporting and criticizing such judgments. Actually "moral judgment" is a blanket term, covering a loosely organized group of types of illocutionary acts—reprimands, behest, injunctions, exhortations, imputations of obligation, *etc.*

In consideration of a particular kind of illocutionary act, say that of a reprimand, there is the locutionary act of uttering a certain expression; there is the perlocutionary act of occasioning some response on the part of the person or persons to whom the reprimand is addressed. There is in addition the illocutionary act, which is not simply uttering an expression, although, to be performed, an appropriate expression must be uttered; thus, the performance of an illocutionary act presupposes the performance of a locutionary act. But, while a perlocutionary act is not performed if no response is brought about, the presence or absence of a response is irrelevant to the identification of an illocutionary act.

In being applied to the analysis of the concept of a moral judgment, these distinctions require consideration of contexts having the following constitutents: (i) a set of linguistic conventions manifested in utterances and inscriptions of various kinds; (ii) a sense of the appropriateness of utterances and inscriptions to occasions; (iii) estimates, particularly as regards the use of moral judgments to modify behavior, of the likely consequences of making moral judgments; *i.e.*, estimates of what perlocutionary acts are likely to attend given illocutionary acts. The analysis of the data of the sociology of moral beliefs in these terms, to the extent that it can be carried out, is an appropriate enlargement of the inquiry into the nature of moral judgments.

The question of basic moral beliefs, or moral presuppositions, must be returned to. Is it possible to identify a set of basic moral values on which there is or could be general agreement? If so, one may come to localize the universality or absoluteness of moral judgments in their reference to these basic values. And even if one could not establish, by analysis of the relevant sociological data, a set of basic moral values as objects of universal belief, one might still argue for such a set of values on scientific grounds, as, for example, John Dewey has done. Such universality or absoluteness is compatible with a multiplicity of moral standards that reflect the particular circumstances of the societies in which they function. These standards are the immediate grounds of praise and blame; and it is possible that they converge in a common general moral values. Thus, the concept of a moral judgment would require a recognition of the level of generality at which a moral evaluation takes place. An absoluteness in foundations is wholly consistent with relativism at the level of the immediate grounds of praise and blame.

It is clear that the identification and defense of basic moral values is essential in this account of a possible resolution of the issue of ethical absolutism over against ethical relativism. One need not adopt an absolutism that implies the irrelevance of sociological data; indeed, they may be the source of the content of a legitimate absolutism. On the other hand, one is not required, in taking seriously the facts of cultural diversity, to adopt a naïve relativism, unable to provide a critique of moral standards.

Notes and References

1. W. T. Stace, *The Concept of Morals*. New York: The Macmillan Co., 1937. Quoted from an excerpt in Paul W. Taylor, *Problems of Moral Philosophy*. Belmont, Calif.: Dickenson Publishing Co., Inc., 1967, pp. 58–59.
2. *Ibid.*, p. 55.
3. *Ibid.*, p. 53.
4. C. D. Broad, *Scientific Thought*. New York: The Humanities Press, Inc., 1923, p. 20.
5. W. P. Alston, *Philosophy of Language*. Englewood Cliffs, N.J.: Prentice-Hall, Inc., 1964, pp. 48–49.